A New Spirituality

Beyond Religion

With Personal Growth That Leads to Spiritual Growth— the Human Being Becomes a Spiritual Being

Patty Paul

IMDEX Publishing
Huntington Beach
California

To Janie and Michael
and the others who
teach me what love is.

To The Reader

This book is neither intended to be, nor presented as, *the* authority on any of the subjects discussed, including physical, mental, emotional, and spiritual health and healing. The reader is encouraged to use their own discernment to form personal judgments and opinions about the value of the information from this and any other source.

Nothing changes until you do.

—Lazaris

CONTENTS

Acknowledgement

In 1985, after reading Shirley MacLaine's *Out on a Limb*, my personal and spiritual quest changed direction. I thank Shirley MacLaine for that important contribution so beneficial to my growth.

There are others I wish to acknowledge who have helped me with *A New Spirituality*, directly and indirectly. Some are mentioned in the "About This Book" section.

I received much-appreciated support and encouragement for writing this book from my mother, Alma Emrick, and from my lifelong friend, Barbara Overton.

Jane Hargitay, Liz Layug, Janet Thomas, Ken White, and Alice Wilson helped to elevate my "resonance" during the period I was writing this book, as we shared in our learning process with dear Shawn Randall and Torah.

Joan Bandelin generously contributed her time and effort as my "reader" and I'm grateful to her for doing so.

Direct assistance toward the production of this book came from Vicky White and Victoria Light, two professionals who helped me immensely.

To all I extend my heartfelt thanks.

About This Book

This book is an expression of my own evolving spirituality formed from my experiences with and beliefs about personal and spiritual growth. The foundation of my spirituality, my truth, is a blending of universal truths known to us all on many levels and the factual knowledge which I've gained from those far wiser than I.

That knowledge has come from teachers who have not only shared their information and wisdom, but who have given me the impetus for further exploration. Those teachers are Lazaris, whom I have heard at numerous seminars over the years, Torah whose classes I have attended for years, and Ophelia, with whom I have had many private consultations, as well as my own personal counselors, especially Aletha.

These unconditionally loving teachers have also inspired me to share the insights I have learned through them, through various other authors, and through my own life experiences. Thus I have written this book.

CHAPTER 1

A New Spirituality

A New Spirituality

*T*he nature and behavior of human beings and humanity are curiosities pondered and debated ever since we humans gained the capacity to do so. There are those who contend that we are born with the basest of instincts and cruelest intent. Unless conditioned by rigid rules of behavior, they believe humanity is destined to writhe in the mud until it destroys itself and everything else. Others believe in the inherent goodness of human nature and that only outside influence twists and distorts that goodness. A diverse range of perceptions lies within those polarities.

In our world there is evidence to support the veracity of every one of those theories. They are contradictions, yet each is a truth; a paradox this book will later explain.

There is one truth about the basic nature of human beings and humanity that is without contradiction. It is that each of us has an *inherent* longing and drive to find and develop our personal connection to our Source and to return to it. To return Home. That is our spirituality and it is a theme found in every civilization throughout history, the thread that connects them. Our spiritual nature is evidenced today, in part, by the existence of some 30,000 religions worldwide.

But religion itself is not spirituality. A religion is a system of beliefs created to contain and control the spiritual flame at its core. The physical structures—some like fortresses—built around the world by various religions are symbolic of the rigid formation of rules and laws of those religious organizations, but they are not manifestations of spirituality.

Spirituality is our personal, free, living, loving relationship with our Source. As we explore and intensify that personal relationship, our awareness expands and we break through the structures of religion and other limiting belief systems—such as atheism. We reach and stretch beyond them. That is spiritual growth.

Spirituality, then, is our unique, loving relationship with our Source and our fundamental urge to reunite with It. Our spirituality is also the *way* in which we develop that relationship, the *means* by which we return Home.

We are propelled on our journey Home, whether in one lifetime or over many, by continually forming and reforming belief systems, ever lighter and freer—having fewer and fewer limitations, breaking through each as our awareness expands.

But awareness of what?

Sooner or later, it is the awareness of our personal power to change our reality by consciously changing ourself and learning how to expedite those changes. That is a major step in our personal growth. This book offers insights and suggestions for achieving personal growth elegantly—without the pain and struggle that got us this far. Personal growth clears our Homeward path, opening the way for spiritual growth.

The awareness we gain will eventually become the knowledge, understanding, and wisdom that this physical world is an illusion, a hologram, and that each of us is an eternal consciousness which exists simultaneously on many levels of reality. This book offers an explanation of the creation and evolution of consciousness for the reader to consider, to sit with, to ponder.

The following chapters explore the changes now occurring in the world. In the consensus reality, many anticipate changes which will precipitate the "second coming" of Christ, a belief that Jesus will literally return to our physical world. A higher truth is that it is *Christ-consciousness* that is returning, that it is compassion, understanding, emotional expression, and unconditional love that is returning —feminine principles for so long devalued and denied in our world.

The essence of Jesus, the man, the essence of Christ-consciousness, the essence of feminine principles—each is an expression of One that humanity turned its back on eons ago, and *She* is returning—though it was never She who left us. The changes in the world are related to Her return.

Ultimately, in our expansion of awareness, we will come to know, once more, the Goddess—and to open to Her love.

Her existence has been denied and memory of Her obliterated over thousands of years of patriarchal civilizations. She did not abandon us, we turned away from Her. But She, and the true God, are returning to help those who so choose create a new world. Not to fix the old world. To create a brand new world in our holographic illusion, as brilliant as we are willing to allow it to be.

The Goddess and true God are the essence of our new spirituality, which, in its intricacy, is the adventure of a lifetime.

Our new spirituality is personal growth which leads to spiritual growth. It is *living* our own spiritual truth, whatever it might be, every day—making it the basis and motivation for everything we do.

Our new spirituality is consciously taking more and more responsibility for creating everything in our life and having personal power and freedom in return. It is discovering our divinity and humanity by finding and establishing self-value.

Our new spirituality is opening to the Goddess and receiving Her love. It is meeting the true, loving God, so unlike the deities created as reflections of the worst in human nature.

Our new spirituality is letting go of the old reality paradigm chained to the past—and opting for a new paradigm focusing on the future.

Our new spirituality is unlimited by inflexible rules based upon domination and fear. It is a faster track for the journey Home.

The chapters which follow are windows, perhaps doors, to concepts outside of the consensus perception of reality and truth. They offer insights into why each of us chose to be born into this lifetime. Insights into how we can become our truer self, our spiritual self.

These chapters are offered as avenues to explore in your spiritual travels.

CHAPTER 2

11

I. Goddess, God, and Their Creation of All That Is

*N*ever wanting to reign alone as singular authority, the Goddess created God from Her imagination, desire, and love, then allowed the endless space that is Her womb to receive His masculine powers of will and action and manifestation.

Through Her allowing and receiving, a harmony of feminine energy and masculine energy occurred, a powerful union was formed...and in that harmony and union, out of the synergy of the Two, was instantly conceived and born All That Is...as He, the seeker of meaning and understanding, and She with Her ability to create and be created, to nurture and be nurtured...as the Two, coming together to conceive and perceive Their creation, asked "Why...?" the first thought in the question "Why am I?"...not yet completed.

And in the asking, an explosion of raw energy of a magnitude beyond comprehension...thrusting exponentially into space She alone can create, downstepping its power into forces and energies, downstepping further as infinite trillions upon trillions of sparks of that energy, downstepping again and again as sparks of sub-atomic particles, sparks of self-generating thought...sparks of consciousness

13

from the mind of God, born from the womb of the Goddess as the unlimited multiplicity of All That Is.[1]

So it began, is now beginning, and will never end, for there is no limitation of time or space in the loving synergy of power and creation that is God/Goddess/All That Is.

In that elegance of partnership and creation of All... born of love and a desire to know more of Themselves... Goddess and God laid a blueprint, a model, for our existence and our spirituality—for the two are inextricably entwined.

The spark of thought from the mind of God is the Spirit with which All is endowed.

Arising from the womb of the Goddess...the Soul... with its depth of feeling and imagination, its love of beauty and harmony which permeates All.

Each spark of consciousness is a piece of God/Goddess/All That Is. Each spark has Spirit and Soul. That is the worth that is *given* and every spark of consciousness has equal worth.

That is our connection to Goddess and God for we each are a spark of consciousness and therefore a piece of Them.

Discovering our worth and *defining* our connection to God/Goddess/All That Is is our spirituality and the path that will lead us Home.

It is never too late to begin the journey Home, for all time is Now.

II. The Evolution of Consciousness

*A*s sparks of raw energy and raw conscious thought were thrust outward from the fusion of God and Goddess in the explosion of creation that fusion produced, individually and uniquely the sparks downstepped their power, downstepped, downstepped, downstepped their power to reach varying levels of stability.

Each, as a self-generating thought, had the capacity to throw out sparks of itself, following the pattern created by God/Goddess/All That Is, and within each spark emitted was the urge to become *more*...was the drive to find the answer to the unfinished question.

Traveling farther and farther away from the Source, each energy unit downstepped as needed to reach the point where it could stabilize. Multiple levels of stabilization were created in that way at varying degrees from the Source.[2]

A minute fraction of infinitely downstepped self-generating consciousness—motivated by the urge to know itself—that portion, by choice, focused its imagination and desire, with expectancy, to create the illusion, the hologram that is our universe.

Ours is a universe of vibrational energies which resonate at compatible frequencies and in that way it is held together, held in harmony in a spirit of cooperation between the energies, between the sparks of consciousness.

All energies within our universe travel by wave action, like the waves produced when pebbles are sprinkled in a pond. Within the universal vibration, other energies downstepped infinitely more times to create what are known as the four lower worlds of physical reality—the Mental Plane where the concept of heaven exists, the Causal Plane where resides all that is possible, the Astral Plane of possibilities, probabilities and dreams, and the Physical Plane of dense manifestation.

Sparks of consciousness enter and exit the universe through a portal that is symbolized by the star Sirius. The portal is a vortex of energy formed by the synergy of Sirius A—the brightest distant star we see from Earth, Sirius B—the dwarf star, and Sirius C—the invisible star. The Sirius vortex is the doorway through which *all* forces and energies enter and exit our universe.

To enter, energy must first downstep to the universal vibrational resonance, then downstep as required to reach the lower levels. To exit, vibrational frequency must be increased—must become higher and lighter—must become *enlightened* until it can transcend the lower planes contained within the universe. Lower does not mean less-than in the judgmental sense. It refers to lower resonance, lower vibrational frequency.

Upon entering the vastness of the newly created universe, the consciousness energies who desired to experience it chose to remain near the entrance, as one might do upon entering a large room. Some—about one third—went to the nearby stellar constellation known as the Pleiades, another third went to the constellation of Orion somewhat farther away, and the remaining third stayed near Sirius.

Our galaxy, the Milky Way, is nearest to the portal of the universe. Our solar system is at the end of the galaxy closest to the portal.

The Physical Plane, including planet Earth and all other domains of physicality, is a hologram in which exist energies such as photons, neutrinos, quarks, and other subatomic particles all vibrating at various levels of frequency. The hologram also contains the space in between them where even more powerful energies and forces reside. The frequencies at which the consciousness energies vibrate escalate downward from ultra-violet light to light to color to ultrasound to sound to aroma to gas to liquid and eventually to solid matter.

Within each level of energy there is an octave of frequencies escalating downward—ultraviolet light resonates at a higher frequency than does orange-colored light, for instance. Ultra-high-frequency, UHF, radio waves resonate at a higher frequency than do the deep tones of a bass drum. Water is comprised of molecules which vibrate at a lower frequency than the gaseous hydrogen and oxygen which combine to produce it, but higher than the ceramic vase in which it might be contained.

Human bodies are made up of molecules which form cells which form bone, tissue, hair, teeth, blood according to the directions encoded into each human's DNA. All of the molecules and cells in a human body are vibrating at the frequency which allows them to perform their function. They stay together in a spirit of cooperation, for this is their way—each is a spark of consciousness—to become more than what they are individually. Each has its own energy and together they create a synergy, a field of energy which acts like a receiver to pick up the focus of the conscious, subconscious, and unconscious minds—the levels collectively called the Mind.

The brain is a hologram in which are manifested the electro-chemical and electro-mechanical functions which keep the body operating. The senses send messages to the brain and it reacts according to the beliefs retained in the Mind. Information from the senses is filtered and adapted by the Mind based upon the beliefs held there. Then attitudes, thoughts, and feelings are produced based upon those beliefs. Personal choices and decisions also stem from them.

Each individual creates their own holographic reality by either *causing* it by their choices and decisions, or by *allowing* it through their attitudes, thoughts, and feelings—all of it born from belief.[3]

How the world is conceived and perceived is a direct result of what beliefs are contained in the conscious, subconscious, and unconscious minds. The unique combination of our beliefs, attitudes, thoughts, feelings, choices, and decisions is the "program" which produces a reality uniquely our own.

It is the focus of Mind, acting like a laser beam, that creates the portion of reality experienced in the hologram. The hologram itself is the creation of the unconscious, subconscious, and conscious minds, and how each of us *experiences* the hologram is a creation of the *focus* of the Mind. In that way, we produce our version of the macrocosm of reality—the world at large—and microcosm of our personal life. It is all an illusion that seems real and tangible to us because we, in our physical body, exist within and are a part of the illusion.

We, as a consciousness, also exist on many other levels beyond the illusory Physical Plane. By acknowledging that fact and expanding our understanding of it, we can change and grow, using what we create in our reality as feedback that tells us how we are doing. There is no need to wait until we move beyond the Physical Plane to review our life, then hope to do better the next time.

Our Higher Self—a level of our consciousness existing far beyond the limitations of the lower planes—chose to expedite its quest for self-knowledge by "sowing" at once hundreds of sparks of consciousness—perhaps thousands— to experience lifetimes on the Physical Plane with the hope that one would awaken to their spirituality in a way that would reunite them with the Higher Self. Each of those sparks of consciousness is an aspect of ourself. Many of those lifetimes we have chosen to consciously experience.

The multiple lives, created out of self-generating thought as downstepped energy from our Higher Self, we know as past lives, parallel lives, future lives, but all exist simultaneously, though in a space or time different from the present focus of our conscious mind. In that sense, our current lifetime is the one we are paying attention to.

We each have one unconscious mind shared by all of our lifetimes and it is a receptacle for *all* of our experience. Each of our lives has its own subconscious mind, a receptacle for current-life experience. We focus our conscious mind on the lifetime in which we find ourself, but our present lifetime may be *influenced* by what is contained in our subconscious mind and unconscious mind. That is how our current-life childhood experiences and past-life experiences have impact on our present reality—if we allow them to.

Focusing our conscious attention on our current life is how we *are* the person living this life. The physical body is not the person, but rather the vehicle we have created in which to experience the lifetime.

Our "light body," as downstepped energy, flows into the hologram of our physical body through a series of ethereal portals; spherical vortices of energy called Chakras. There are several sets of Chakra centers, with seven Chakras in each set, but perhaps the most significant—at least the most commonly known—is the set of seven Chakras which exist within our holographic torso and head.

Each of the body Chakras relates to certain parts of the physical body and concerns particular mental, physical, emotional, and spiritual aspects of the being. They are linked to our endocrine system and therefore impact and are impacted by the function of glands located near them.

The first torso Chakra is situated near the tailbone, from back to front. It is red in color and the size of a fist. The first Chakra relates to issues of physical, emotional, and mental security and safety. It affects the posterior region, the hands, ankles, feet and wrists and is related to the spleen and kidney functions.

The second torso Chakra appears in the genital area and is related to the testes or ovary glands. It is orange in color and about the size of a quarter. Creativity and plea-sure—including sexual pleasure—are impacted by the energy flowing through this Chakra. The entire pelvic region is related to the second Chakra.

The third Chakra of the torso set involves the emotions —emotional impact on the being and their emotional impact on others. It is a buttery yellow center, eight to ten inches in diameter, located in the solar plexus and involves the stomach, upper digestive tract and pancreas gland.

The fourth, or heart Chakra lies mid-chest behind the sternum bone. It is emerald green in color and about four inches across. The heart Chakra involves issues of love— self-love and love for others—including giving, receiving, and being loved. It is related to the thymus gland.

Below the Adam's Apple, behind the indentation in the

"v" of the collarbone, is the fifth Chakra. It is a deep sky blue and about the size of a half-dollar. The energy which flows in and out of the fifth Chakra has to do with communication—what is let in and what is expressed regarding all of the issues connected to the other Chakras. It relates to the larynx and thyroid gland.

The sixth Chakra, located behind the forehead above the nose and between the eyes, is royal purple in color and near the size of a quarter. It is known as the third eye by some and it relates to intuition and the psychic connection to the higher realms. The pituitary gland, which regulates the functions of the other glands in the body, is impacted by the sixth Chakra.

Below the soft spot on the top of the head, in the interior of the brain, lies the seventh Chakra. It is a pinpoint of light and in its condensed mass it is very powerful. The seventh Chakra, violet-white in color, is linked to the pineal gland located in that area of the brain. It is our portal to the higher spiritual levels. The pineal gland controls the function of the pituitary gland and also senses light outside of the body. When open, it receives *enlightenment* from the spiritual realms. The seventh Chakra/pineal gland is the actual third eye of the holographic brain.

Light-body consciousness enters and leaves the holographic body through the Chakra centers at the birth and death of the being.

As we downstepped our energy to the Physical Plane, first as a spark of thought from our Higher Self—which was a spark from its Higher Self—the spark became a photon of light. The photon, seeking to become more, became a sub-subatomic particle, which became a subatomic particle, which became an atom, which became a molecule and in that way, downstepping our vibration, becoming denser and denser, eventually we chose to become solid matter—a major leap for a molecule.

Our choice brought about a most momentous shift and we became dense matter in the physical realm we were closest to and therefore the one we could aspire to. We entered the mineral kingdom. We did so to experience and to learn about the thing called physicality. Whether as a grain of beach sand, a mountain high, or any other form within the realm, we experienced the mineral kingdom for as long as we desired before deciding to move on. The mineral kingdom offered entry into the physical world but limited opportunity for growth.

The next level was the plant kingdom, with more potential for growth—in a lineal way upward and downward, and outward as well—with feelings and sensitivities not found in the mineral realm. Our existence there may have been as a tree in a forest, as a day lily, as a blade of grass. It was whatever we chose it to be for the experience we sought.

When we chose to leave the plant kingdom—ever motivated by the urge to become more—we advanced to the animal kingdom. That was a giant step into a realm of senses, instincts, awareness, and movement not possible in the lower kingdoms.

Through an evolutionary progression of lifetimes within the animal realm, we were able to grow in consciousness to the point where we were ready to enter the human kingdom—but in its most primitive state.

We lived lifetimes as what could be called *human animals*.[4] Lifetimes where survival was the driving force and all that mattered. Animal instinct was replaced with ego to act as a deliverer of messages from our outer world through our senses.

Eventually, in a primitive existence, something happened. A thought, an awareness, a feeling that there *has* to be something *more* than simply surviving day to day. With that new insight, we became a human *being*.[5]

Driven now by a motivation to learn of the more, depth and meaning were added to mere existence and our journey changed direction.

In our first *directional*[6] lifetime, we turned Homeward.

CHAPTER 3

Discovering Personal Destiny

Discovering Personal Destiny

*A*fter each lifetime, in our retreat from the physical world, we find our way to the Causal Plane where we review the last incarnation to learn more about ourself from it. Before entering a new lifetime, we choose personal goals for change and growth as seven focuses to be an agenda for the upcoming life.

The first two focuses are the same for each of us in every life—to *learn to consciously create success* and to *learn how to have fun*[7] as we experience our reality. The remaining five we select as the unique combination of issues we wish to work on for the purpose of spiritual growth. Perhaps it is to take back our power we've given away to others. Or perhaps to process and release anger at men, or women, or authority, which has been harbored in other lifetimes.

Life focuses, or destiny as some would say, are chosen out of free will, not assigned. They are selected depending upon the emphasis one wants to have in the upcoming lifetime. If it is to be an easygoing life, perhaps the focuses would be on less knotty subjects. On the other hand, if it is decided that the lifetime shall be one of significant growth and many old issues that were previously swept under the rug are to be addressed, a full load of weighty issues might be put on the agenda.

Then, in the spirit of universal cooperation and harmony, the conscious being reaches agreements with others who have compatible agendas, to come together at appropriate times in the next incarnation so that each can work on their particular issues. Those who are to be parents and offspring come together by agreement in this way. The parents are the avenue for entry into the new physical life and also co-creators of the environment which will provide a mutual opportunity to deal with focuses.

To exemplify how this works, say that one who wishes to deal with a personal propensity for martyrhood (see pg. 107) —a blockage to spiritual growth—might arrange to have many children in the next life. Or dependent parents. Or an unfaithful spouse. The environment for martyrhood is established and it is for the individual to reach the level of awareness where they can *realize* that they are in martyrhood, *own the fact that they have consciously created the reality* so that they could indulge in the payoffs provided by martyrhood, *forgive themself for creating the reality*, and decisively *choose to be different.* That is how growth comes about.

Upon entering the new lifetime, all will be forgotten of course, so beforehand, we set forth clues to the issues we wish to deal with by choosing the precise moment and place of our birth. The configuration of the stars and planets in our holographic heavens at the time and space in which we are born will tell us through astrology what energies we have selected to encounter and work with in the lifetime. That is the value of a natal astrological horoscope.

As we deal with our obstacles, process our blockages, and fulfill our initial focuses, however, we change and so does our self-determined destiny. Neither the stars, nor planets, nor any other forces in our universe have power over us, unless we freely give it.

Though we enter the physical plane through a veil of amnesia, in infancy and early childhood we *are* more connected to our pre-incarnation existence in the non-physical world. Young children are more of their real self and more sensitive to the spiritual nature of all that is.

The Soul may enter the body of the unborn fetus or it may wait until up to three days following birth. If it has not entered the physical body by that time, the conscious entity has changed its mind—and the infant body dies.

Birth into physicality is a traumatic event for a conscious being previously free of such limitations.

As the infant develops into child, and the child into adolescent, beliefs are formed, attitudes, thoughts, and feelings are developed out of its interaction with parents, siblings, teachers, religion, and all of the other elements of the consensus reality. That is the environmental influence that so molds a being and its relationship to others and to the world.

Most often, personal and spiritual growth is stunted by twisted and limiting beliefs and by feelings unexpressed and stuffed away.

It is by discovering what is inside us and dealing with the source and the reasons for those limiting beliefs and stuffed feelings—and also the impact they have on our reality—that we can be free of them to grow personally as a human being. Personal growth clears the way for spiritual growth. The human being becomes a spiritual being.

Getting to know ourself in that way, taking responsibility for what we find, then changing within is how we change our reality, how we *consciously create* our reality. When we know how to do that, we can then learn how to consciously co-create with our Higher Self.

Although we decide upon focuses before we enter a lifetime, we are free to modify them at any time. Some create too difficult a path to follow—too much hardship—because they have the mistaken belief in karmic law. Karma is not a law, it is a choice. Everything is personal choice.

God/Goddess/All That Is loves each of us unconditionally. They never say No. Can we have unlimited love, fun, and success? Yes. Can we have misery, pain, and degradation? Yes. They enthusiasticly support us when what we seek is for our highest spiritual good, *with harm to none*. We *alone* create the negativity in our lives.

It is by learning to create our reality, then to co-create it with one who is *more*, not better-than, but *more* than we are, that we utilize the power of Goddess and God that is contained in the minute spark of Them which we are. As above, so below.

Focuses can be changed as we fulfill them or as we see that there is another way to learn and to grow. We can always learn any lesson through love. There is no need to learn through pain.

Eastern religions and philosophies approach spiritual growth as a slow process, born of lifetimes of self-denial, poverty, suffering, and hardship. Other religions teach that we are weak, powerless, or inherently bad and must live our lives in subservience, self-sacrifice, and guilt. They are merely belief systems with severe limitations.

Where human life is more valued, where there is more self-love, there is less suffering and deprivation.

When we leave a physical lifetime, we take our personality, beliefs, and emotions with us—for they are the only things real in our physical illusion, and we continue to create our reality out of them on the other side. If we die hold-

ing severely limiting beliefs or intense, unexpressed, feelings, if we make that transition with our blockages to
growth intact, we may create a hellish reality on the Astral
Plane—until we are ready to change. Some who have
passed to the other side remain so closely connected to the
physical world—often by the trauma of their death and
intense feelings surrounding that trauma—that they are
indeed tethered to it.

There is always opportunity for growth on every level,
and there are helpers—counselors, guides, angels, beings of
light—to facilitate our growth. On the higher levels, learning continues, as it does on all planes, but it is done consciously. Entities are aware that All is a classroom. That is
forgotten when we enter physicality. To discover it once
again and then to take responsibility for creating our reality
is what empowers us to be *conscious* creators now.

To know ourself in that way, to know our power and
how to change reality by changing within is how we
become whole—how we become one with our real self. It
is from that place of wholeness that we can truly express our
spirituality. Spirituality, our personal relationship with God/
Goddess/All That Is, is developed as our unique experience
and communication with the higher realms. The more
responsibility for our reality we assume, the faster we grow.

A child lacks the capacity to be responsible for creating
their reality, although, ironically, up to the age of about ten
years they believe that they *cause* everything that affects
them. Much of the self-hatred and shame that is buried
within us comes from this early period. It is for the adult
who was once that child to take responsibility for uncover-
ing the shame, anger, fear, self-pity, hatred, and other emotions submerged in the shadow self, and to process them
out in the light. Once expressed in whichever way is most

appropriate, they are to then be released, and the self forgiven for harboring those feelings. Then a conscious decision to change is to be made, followed by appropriate choices. A new reality will be the result.

It is never too late to do this processing, and it is the processing that clears the obstructions from the path so that spiritual growth can occur.

The reason we have chosen to learn on the Physical Plane is that growth can be much more accelerated here because we get so much feedback that lets us know how we are progressing. We also have the cushions of time and space in our physical world that provide the opportunity to make mistakes, to learn from them, and to change. Our successes let us know we are on the right path.

Our spirituality, our connection to God/Goddess/All That Is, is also reflected by the state of our health. As blockages interfere with spiritual growth, that interference often manifests in the physical body. When we are disconnected from fulfilling the focuses we set for ourselves, distracted from our journey Home, illness or injury is often the result.

It is the seeking and the finding of our focuses, our destiny, that is our link to God/Goddess/All That Is and when a disruption occurs between the seeking and the finding, the physical body often is the messenger that tells us something is amiss. Sometimes it is our Higher Self who uses the physical body in that way to get our attention, to get us to slow down and take a look at something that needs tending.

The clues that the body gives us are quite overt. Cancer is often caused by suppressed anger that one feels hopeless about, stored for so long that the cells, themselves, must process it. Anger always gets processed, one way or another. We *always* take responsibility for creating our reality. It's done either consciously or unconsciously.

Cancer is one way responsibility is taken *unconsciously*, one way suppressed anger gets expressed. Where the cancer occurs in the body is a clue to what the anger is about.

One way to *consciously* take responsibility for the anger that's there is to process it in a "hate" letter (never shown to anyone else) written with great emotion, really *feeling* the emotion as it's written. Then, when the letter is completed, when it *feels* complete, and after re-reading it several times, it is destroyed with the *intent* and *feeling* of releasing the anger. Often it is our inner child or adolescent who needs to express their repressed emotions in this way.

Self-love, unexpressed, unreceived, denied, can be as physically devastating as unexpressed anger. Heart problems may result. Lack of self-love threatens our very existence as human beings.

Other feedback from our reality indicates which issues we have chosen to address in our lifetime in addition to the two which are common to all.

We can identify those other five issues by looking carefully at the significant events of our life. Beginning with childhood, selecting perhaps four or five events which evoked strong emotions—whether we suppressed them or not—from birth to five years of age, five events from six to ten years of age, ten to thirteen, and so on. A pattern will emerge which points to particular repetitive emotions, situations, relationships—like fear, loneliness, martyrhood, abandonment, betrayal, victimhood, abuse, need to control. They are the clues we are looking for. All of us experience those emotions and circumstances from time to time, but when they are repeated frequently enough to set a lifelong pattern—then they hold significance as focuses we programmed ourself to deal with.

Besides martyrhood, lack of self love, and suppression of anger, there are other blockages to growth. Victimhood, self-pity, self-importance (feeling better-than or less-than other people), self-righteous anger, blame, guilt, and clinging to the past are some of them. Lack of self-trust, of self-esteem, or of self-confidence are others. It is important to realize that we do not have to continue any pattern, that we have the power to end it whenever we choose. For instance, when a victim stops being a victim, the whole dynamic of victim/bully changes. In that sense, it is the *victim* who is in control.

What we see as unwanted obligations can either be changed into preferences or can be dropped altogether. If we make the decision to end an obligation responsibly, from our adult self with the intention of "harm to none," that decision is a growth step.

There are positive aspects of ourself which also emerge as we look at our life from this new perspective. We all have strengths, talents, and gifts. Many times we have chosen them as life focuses to discover or expand them.

Creativity and productivity, leadership and communication, love and intimacy, empathy and caring, discernment, courage, forgiveness, self-trust, a sense of humor, imagination and will, passion and compassion are personal strengths [8] to be appreciated and developed.

By reviewing our life and identifying the patterns we see, the focuses we selected pre-birth become apparent. It is necessary to be brutally honest with ourself regarding both the positive and the negative aspects we identify. A trustworthy friend may be of help here.

As we take more and more responsibility for creating our reality, there is more and more help available to us through unseen friends. One of them is our Higher Self. It is the higher vibrational frequency of ourself who cast out numbers of lives in the hope of having one who finds its spiritual path Home. Reuniting spiritually with our Higher Self and then co-creating reality is the next level of our growth.

We also have unseen counselors, or guardian angels, or spirit-guides. No matter what we call them, we each have at least two, one personified in male form and the other in female form, who have always been with us in all of our lifetimes. Occasionally one or the other may have been physically present. They will assist us if we ask for help, as will our Higher Self—providing what we ask for is in line with our positive growth.

It is possible to contact these entities in meditation unless a belief stands in the way.

Beliefs are one of the boundaries which limit us. It is possible to expand our boundaries and changing beliefs is the primary way we can directly change our reality. Beliefs and how to change them are discussed in Chapter 5.

When we make the conscious choice to expand our spiritual awareness and growth, a light goes on, quite literally, which attracts those beings who love us and who are devoted to helping us in our quest for spiritual truth—our personal truth.

By relaxing in a quiet place, closing our eyes and doing whatever feels right to become more physically at ease, while also setting our conscious mind adrift, we can imagine our own private safe place and, as we desire to, we can invite our Higher Self and/or any other unseen friends, including our inner child and adolescent, to meet with us there. Some may be able to visualize them quite clearly, others not at all. It does not matter so long as we *sense* their presence.

We may wish to ask our unseen friend what is standing in the way of our getting something specific or general that we want. After silencing the voice of our negative ego (see pg. 110) by saying NO (we can ask our Higher Self to help us) and by allowing ourself to *receive* the answer, we can create a loving and valuable source of help for consciously creating our physical reality.

We can also meditatively return to a safe haven we knew as child or adolescent, meeting with the inner child and adolescent there and encouraging them to express their pent-up thoughts and feelings to bring about a healing.

Many books and audio tapes are available on this type of creative, or "working," meditation which involves the imagination and the subconscious and unconscious minds.

Imagination is the voice of our Soul. The more vivid, deep, and rich our imagination, the more we allow our Soul to speak to us.

Using our imagination and feeling desire with the expectation of success, we can create any reality we want—if our beliefs, attitudes, thoughts, feelings, choices, and decisions are compatible with that reality.

The fulfillment of our seven focuses, our destiny, is the personal fulfillment we seek in each lifetime. It satisfies our deepest needs, known to us on a cellular level. When what we seek to create is in line with our focuses, we cannot fail.

CHAPTER 4

Masculine and Feminine Energies and Their Impact on Reality

Masculine and Feminine Energies and Their Impact on Reality

*G*od/Goddess/All That Is are the model of how masculine and feminine energies, working in harmonious partnership, create a synergy that is more powerful than its separate components. Both masculine and feminine energies are found in everything that exists. They have nothing to do with sex or gender, but everything to do with powerful creation. It is from the synergy of those energies that All was created and it is through the synergy of those energies within that we each can powerfully create *our* reality.

It is the *seeking* of balance, for they are fluid and fluctuating energies and will never be statically balanced, that will produce a harmonious world. Such harmony has emerged from time to time in our world's history.

The Earth, as a life-supporting planet, is about two billion years old and human beings, distinguished from their human animal predecessors, first appeared about 100,000 years ago. The human experience has been relatively brief here.

There were ancient civilizations of Lemuria[9] and Atlantis[10] which laid the foundation for what was to come.

LEMURIA

Lemurian civilizations were, for the most part, highly advanced, highly spiritual. Lemuria, a continent in the peaceful sea now called Pacific, was the domain of the Goddess. It was the introduction and the expression of Her influence, the introduction and expression of feminine energy, into and upon our physical world.

Lemuria was a land cloaked in fine mist, making luminescent the colors of flowers and greenery and light.

The northeasterly territory was mountainous timber country, with lumbermen's houses cantilevered above steep and darkly forested slopes. In the eastern coastal section lay rolling hills and farmland. Uninhabited islands lay offshore.

The south coastal area was mining territory, and flat farmland extended along the westernmost coast.

Small villages, like those now in Switzerland, were sprinkled throughout the outlying areas.

The central region was encircled by sheer cliffs fronting tall mountains, thus separating it from the outer territories. Within the interior lay lush tropical forests out of which rose, like huge columns, buttes of land 200 to 500 feet high and flat on top. Some stood in clusters, others alone.

Upon the buttes were built cities of wood, stone, and stucco—spiritual learning centers devoted to instructing the healers, the speakers, the witnesses, the teachers, and the dreamers. The only access to the top of a butte was by teleportation from its base. Using their tools of imagination, desire, and expectancy in meditation, those who were meant to be there were able to reach the teaching cities.

Periodically, certain children—guided by dreams, by inner knowing, or by teachers who were drawn to them—would make their way to the cities for instruction. After five, ten, or twenty years—whatever was appropriate—many would go forth into the lowlands to share what they had learned.

The roofs of the high cities were covered with crystals. Rising tall above the misty forests, they shone brilliantly in the sun—Crystal Cities they were called.

The many civilizations of Lemuria evolved culturally and spiritually until there came a time when Lemurians knew their growth on the Physical Plane was completed. Each had a choice of transcending to the higher realms or returning to the Physical Plane. Many, out of love for humanity, opted to return to begin anew in lifetime after lifetime—each time searching once again for their spiritual path Home.

Those who chose to return would always have available, in their unconscious mind, the knowledge and the spiritual light of Lemuria so that they might re-discover that wisdom and one day shine that light in a darkened world

Around 70,000 to 60,000 BC, the land of Lemuria evaporated into the mist. Lemurian crystals had been pro-grammed with knowledge and seeded in the world, just as the returnees would be. A reflection of Lemurian energy is found in the cultures of Polynesia, and the earliest cultures of what is now the Orient, India, Pacific aborigine, and American Indian.

ATLANTIS

The three civilizations of Atlantis were expressions of mas-culine energy that became imbalanced.

In each of those civilizations, technology eventually was valued over human life. Each of the civilizations reached the heights of great technological advancement, but because of corruption and indifference to human values—and a failure to assume personal responsibility for changing the reality—each was destroyed by natural disasters. It was not nature's attack, not God's wrath, but the reality Atlantinians created to let themselves know the direction they had chosen was taking them off course on their journey Homeward.

1st Civilization

The continent of Atlantis was located in the northern hemisphere, in the Atlantic sea. The upper third of the continent was separated from the lower two-thirds by a deep and wide valley through which flowed a major river. Beginning about 50,000 BC, primitive but homeostatically-balanced groups of humans, who essentially killed and slept, existed there.

As some of those human animals evolved into human beings, there developed over time a civilization located in the southeastern coastal region, which was separated from the rest of the continent by a range of mountains. That section eventually became the City of Atlantis, hundreds of miles long.

Other cities in the area were likewise protected from the more primitive interior region. As this first Atlantinian civilization developed, it became more and more technology oriented, finally valuing technology over people's rights.

The destruction of the first civilization of Atlantis was brought about during the 41st millennium BC by a series of earthquakes which produced a chain reaction of fires. Many nuclear energy plants, stadiums, and other significant structures had been built over fault lines. Most inhabitants did not survive.

2nd Civilization

The continent of Atlantis was split into two land masses by tectonic action during the first destruction. The upper third of the continent split off and remained a primitive island. On the lower portion, once again from rudimentary origins, there evolved a civilization more advanced than any the world has known.

The downfall of this second Atlantinian civilization was brought about by political corruption and by power for its own sake.

The corrupt government was held together by martial law and martial law was used to maintain the level of mediocrity that prevailed.

Graft paid to allow development of land lying over earthquake fault lines helped to set up the conditions for destruction.

The combination of martial law and governmental corruption brought about the destruction of the second civilization of Atlantis around 28,200 BC

The internal corruption was manifested outwardly as natural disasters—volcanic eruptions, earthquakes, fires, tidalwaves. Few survived. But some, in boats and rafts carried along by gulf streams, were able to make their way to other lands where they formed small pockets of civilization.

3rd Civilization

The second destruction reduced the upper land mass of Atlantis to many small islands and the lower portion to a grouping of larger islands. The upper islands remained primitive and mostly uninhabited because of their isolation.

As civilization evolved once more in the lower area, a new City of Atlantis was established on a chain of islands.

The third civilization also became highly advanced. There were automobiles, though they were impractical because of island life, and there were powerboats. There were skyscrapers of glass and chrome, and structures we would recognize as Greek-style architecture. People had colorful hot-air balloons for extended travel. Some flew around the world and were aware of the barbarians and primitives who lived in other places.

With the advancements, however, came a loss of respect for human dignity and for human value, for the emphasis was once more on technology at the expense of human beings. The consensus had not developed their spirituality; they had no sense of personal fulfillment. People lost hope and they forgot how to dream, how to imagine.

Poverty, homelessness, and drug addiction were widespread. Those afflicted were the "forgotten ones." People were warehoused. Old people were exiled to one island. Prostitutes were sent to a separate, guarded island. Derelicts and drunks were shipped—out of sight—to another. Water supplies on any island could be polluted to kill the residents and reclaim the land.

There were those, outside of the consensus, who tried in vain to bring about reform. They included an underground of metaphysicians who opposed the horror, the damage, and the destruction that was done to the forgotten ones. They set up half-way houses to help the homeless and the addicts—many of them very young. Some spoke out against the government, considered a treasonous act. But they did not know that they had the personal power to change the reality. They gave up their power to blame, to righteous anger, to martyrhood, to self-pity. In that way, they *allowed* the reality to be what it was.

The final destruction by earthquakes, tidalwaves, breaking of natural gas lines, and resulting pollution occurred about 10,800 BC. Those cataclysms obliterated what was left of the Atlantinian continent. This time, however, many more escaped. Certain ones had anticipated the coming destruction and had prepared for it. Some of them left before the disasters began, others left at the first signs.

The survivors were like the seeds of their civilization. In boats, they followed the currents and spread out in various directions. Groups of refugees landed on the shores of western Europe, Africa, the Middle East, and the Far East. Some rafted southwest on currents which took them to the Yucatan peninsula, barren and inhospitable. From there they migrated to the Americas. The great Mayan, Incan, and Aztec civilizations arose from Atlantinian origins.

Some refugees huddled together in small communities, eventually becoming extinct. Others integrated and had great impact on the cultures with which they merged. The Druidic cultures of Great Britain and France emanated from Atlantinian influence.

Pockets of Atlantinian survivors who had the ability to work with laser beams, used extensively in Atlantis, were the basis of later myths about Greek Gods.

Other Atlantinian survivors found their way to Sumer, now Iraq. Because of their influence, Sumerian culture became very advanced. It contributed to discoveries made in Egypt. Egyptian and Sumerian calendars were both based upon the rotation of the star system Sirius because Atlantinians knew of its spiritual significance and therefore its great importance to humanity.

July 23rd of each year begins the period of 55 days when Sirius is closest to the Earth and its vortex of energy opens. Calendars of Sumer, Egypt, and other ancient cultures began on what we know as that date.

Certain Atlantinians went directly to the area now Egypt, but because they loved to travel, they moved on. The came to be known as Gypsies. Other refugees migrated to Egypt from areas of the Middle East where they first landed.

Egyptian pyramids were built with Atlantinian technology using sound waves to pulverize gigantic stone blocks into pebbles, later to be re-assembled in place by again using sound waves. The pyramids were constructed so that when Sirius is closest to the Earth, Sirius's light would shine through windows designed for that purpose.

Pyramids of similar design are found today in the far flung parts of the world where Atlantinians migrated. The refugees also brought with them crystals, programmed with knowledge (crystals hold energy and also give off energy when tapped or rubbed), and buried or scattered them in the areas they inhabited. They also brought their spiritual and religious beliefs which included the worship of the Goddess and God.

The migration of Atlantinian survivors produced a dispersion of advanced knowledge around the world. The standing stones, pyramids, temples, and crystals found throughout the world today evidence the influence of Atlantis.

OTHER EARLY CIVILIZATIONS

For tens of thousands of years in the areas now known as Europe, the Middle East, India, Asia, and some other parts of the world, there were small pockets of agrarian cultures which existed in peace and harmony with each other and with the universe. They had a spiritual connection with nature—with the elements, with the mineral, plant, and animal realms—and with the heavens. And they knew of the Goddess then. They who lived in those small societies lived in dominion with their world. Each grouping had its own religion, its own spirituality. "Pagan" means country. These were pagan religions whose followers believed in the rights of each person to believe as they chose so long as no harm was done to others. They did not seek to dominate nature or each other, just as the Goddess and true God have no desire to dominate or oppress.

Relics of those cultures, some identified by archeologists as dating back to 24,000 BC or earlier, indicate the peaceful, egalitarian nature of ones who lived then. Religious alters found in each home indicate that spirituality was part of daily life.

There was no apparent class distinction or gender or age discrimination. Certain older women were often buried with generous amounts of art objects and jewelry. It is supposed that they held honored positions but they were not buried in segregated grounds.[11]

Around 4,400 to 4,300 BC, horse riding invaders from a male dominant culture residing in southern Russia swept into the European areas occupied by the peaceful agrarian cultures.[12]

The rise of patriarchy in southern Russia has been linked to the domestication of the horse and other large animals indigenous to that region. Men had the physical strength required to dominate and tame large animals.[13]

As archeological findings disclose, when the invaders on horseback struck central Europe, the peaceful, agrarian, matrilineal societies living there began to change.

Over the next 1,400 years, two more such invasions occurred which transformed the makeup of the resident cultures and which also brought about migrations of people into the south of Europe and the Mediterranean area.[14]

Burial grounds from those later periods reveal that the graves of high ranking men, whose wives and children were often interred with them, were separated from the graves of those with lower status. Weapons of war and bodies with mortal wounds violently inflicted, further indicate the nature of the later patriarchal cultures.[15]

Similar changes occurred in cultures existing in other parts of the world—Asia, India, the Americas. What had been peaceful, nature loving societies, became infiltrated and dominated by patriarchal forces.

Whenever an imbalance of masculine and feminine energies within individuals and humankind occurs, that imbalance brings about a shift in consciousness which manifests in the physical world. The history of Atlantis is an example of what can happen. The state of our present world is another.

FEMALE CHAUVINISM

A preponderance of feminine energy or too little masculine energy creates certain conditions which produce particular symptoms—messages that something is off kilter.

Too much feminine energy, or too little masculine, can produce a hatred for men and for masculine energy and an over-valuation of feminine energy. That is female chauvinism.[16]

It can produce an effeteness of unfulfilled dreams that disintegrate into wishful thinking and self-delusion. The feminine imbalance can create the inability to put content into form—having knowledge but no way of implementing it.

It can limit the expression of feeling, with emotions harbored in order to continue blame, righteous anger, and self-pity. It can produce manipulation that turns malevolent, evil. It can rob us of the ability to act and, finally it can lead to the denial of our self—the destruction of Self.

MALE CHAUVINISM

When masculine energy outweighs feminine energy, which has been the case worldwide—with minor exceptions—for the last 4,000 years, the result is an over-valuation of things masculine and a devaluation of the feminine. That imbalance produces male chauvinism.[17]

Male chauvinism regards anything which is an aspect of feminine energy, such as compassion, nurturing, emotional expression, receiving, allowing, being, imagination, and creativity, as inferior and weak. As something to be avoided and reviled.

Competition and comparison, appearance and performance are all that is important in a male-dominated world.

Masculine principles of action and will, without the balance of emotional feeling; creating form with little attention to content and context; image as all-important; domination and control, rather than dominion and co-creation; people functioning as de-humanized acquisition machines; alienation from the world; victimhood and self-pity—these are the conditions we create in our personal reality and in the world at large when there is too much masculine energy or too little feminine.

It is the balancing of masculine and feminine energies *within* that produces a balanced and harmonious world without. It is the pronounced imbalance which produces discord.

Through the ages which followed the demise of the egalitarian, nature-loving cultures, there was a steady rise in the resonant level of male energy. It eventually overpowered all that was feminine. That lopsided imbalance is the foundation for the male chauvinism prevalent in modern civilization. There are few exceptions to that imbalance which has manifested literally as a man's world.

The principles of chauvinism—which include domination, control, and singular authority—have been programmed into the subconscious and unconscious minds of all men and women in modern civilization and those principles distort our perceptions of reality.

We have each contributed to the creation of our world as an expression of male chauvinism. Each of us has chosen to be either a man or a woman about the same number of times in our many incarnations, just as we have chosen where it is we will be born and into what circumstances.

As women, we have given away our power in a tradeoff for being taken care of, or out of lethargy, or simply for sex. We have chosen power without responsibility by seeking it through a man—any man—instead of developing our own. We have willingly abandoned our ideals and goals and spirituality in order to attract and hold a man. We have sought to fulfill our own masculine energies through our relationships with men and have always been disappointed. As women, we are the ones who pass along to our children the male chauvinistic standards of our societies.

As men, we have opted for domination and control and have eagerly oppressed others to gain it and keep it. We have discarded our feminine energy because we thought it inferior and have been left empty without it. We looked to women to provide us with what we disowned in ourself and punished them when they could not.

In a man's world, powerless women get to take payoffs like blame, righteous anger, victimhood, martyrhood, self-pity, self-importance—feeling better-than or less-than men. Men take the same payoffs because they perceive that all the responsibilities of the world lie solely on their shoulders and they feel overburdened.

Male chauvinism, while dominating and devaluing feminine energy, is fearful of it. Chauvinism says there can be only one supreme authority. It suppresses feminine energy, for to allow it is to give it power and that is too threatening to singular rule.

In truth, it is the synergy of masculine energy and feminine energy in equal measure that produces power—personal power and powerful societies.

When Goddess and God joined their energies in partnership to create All That Is, they provided the model of how we can bring forth the internal masculine and feminine energies and create from that source of power.

Competition and comparison are basic to male chauvinism. Appearance and performance are elemental too. Over-valuing them, as we do in our world, keeps us at a superficial level in our relationship with ourself and with others and stands in the way of personal growth and spiritual growth.

As we seek and develop our internal feminine energies of *imagination*, *desire*, and *feeling*; of the *ability to conceive*—not only children, but new ideas, new *content* for our reality, and *to perceive* with all of our senses what we have created; as we draw upon our feminine qualities to *nurture and be nurtured*, to *give and receive* and to *allow*; as we *seek balance and harmony* in our reality; and learn how to *be* [18]—as we elicit those qualities from within, we bring forth the feminine energies within the man or woman that we are.

As we activate our internal masculine energies of powerfully *manifesting* through *will* and *action*; of *creating form* then *dynamically creating out of the form*; of *refocusing energy to produce new form*, new structure; as we draw upon our masculine qualities to *search for the meaning and understanding* of what we have created; to *provide* for and to *protect* our creation, and to learn how to *do* [19]—as we develop those qualities within us we draw forth the masculine aspects of ourself, as woman or man.

To effectively utilize our internal masculine and feminine energies, we weave them together to form a powerful matrix of creation. Our feminine principles of imagination and desire are integrated with our masculine will and action to dynamically manifest what we imagine and desire, allowing ourself to feel our emotions as they arise.

Having the ability to conceive new ideas and new content for our reality, we create form, structure, to hold the content of our reality. With all of our senses, we perceive the new form and new content we have created—learning about ourself from it, then dynamically re-create out of the form, by refocusing energy, to produce new form, new structure.

Throughout the process, we nurture ourself and our creation and allow ourself to be nurtured by others; we both give and receive.

We search for meaning and understanding from what we have created, at once seeking balance and harmony within ourself so as to manifest them in our creation. We provide for and protect what we have created—and from the whole process, we learn how to *do* and how to *be* as the powerful creator—thereby becoming more of who we really are...a spark of God/Goddess/All That Is.

Masculine and feminine energies are fluid and fluctuating. Perfect balance is never found. It is the *seeking* of balance that creates harmony, and it is the harmony which creates power.

The gender we have chosen for ourself in this lifetime is the clue that tells us which energy to start with as we bring them both forth and weave them together. Our gender is the clue that tells us which energy first needs to be explored and understood in dealing with our life focuses.

CHAPTER 5

I. Belief and Religion

*O*ur personal belief system is our personal truth. For each of us, it is The Truth. It is the nature of spirituality, a dynamic living energy comprised of both masculine and feminine aspects, to seek belief systems and structures—to establish religions—as an expression of its masculine component which seeks form.[20] It is also the nature of spirituality to break free of belief systems, stretching and reaching beyond them—as an expression of its feminine ability to create new space and to conceive new content.[21]

Spiritual *growth* is about creating and expanding belief systems, then finally transcending them—while always reaching for the Highest Truth.

The Highest Truth is the one with the least limitations.[22]

BELIEF

Some of our beliefs are borne with us as we are born into the physical world. The rest we develop over time as we absorb input from outside sources. The influence of our environment molds our beliefs. Our reality is created from them. How we relate to the world is expressed through our

57

thoughts and feelings which flow from our attitudes—all sourced in our beliefs.

The belief system uniquely our own forms a structure in which we live our life. The more restrictive our beliefs, the more limited we are within the structure. Our beliefs also form the core of our identity, that's why we feel threatened and defensive if it is suggested that certain of our beliefs may be detrimental or faulty.

In infancy, all information comes from outside sources. How we are treated by mother, father, siblings, and others near us—their attitudes toward us and what we hear them say—forms the basis of what we believe about ourself and the world.

An unborn child, even in its earliest fetal stages, is impacted by the beliefs, attitudes, thoughts, and emotions of its mother. An unwanted child will be born with a sense of rejection because its mother conveyed that message during her pregnancy.

Teachers, religion, peers, the media, government, and other "authorities" which establish the consensus, contribute to a child's belief system.

As adolescents, with the chaos of raging hormones and fearing the relentless approach of adulthood, we grab onto *absolute* kinds of beliefs—black or white, always/never beliefs—in order to stabilize our turbulent lives. With the intensity of adolescent energy behind the beliefs adopted, they become mentally chiseled in stone and stored in the vault of our subconscious mind.

Bigotry and prejudice are most often established in adolescence.

Core beliefs from infancy, childhood, and adolescence are carried with us into adulthood. Those buried in the subconscious mind become Law. The conscious mind may forget, but the subconscious never does.

The subconscious mind is a faithful servant. It delivers a reality consistent with the beliefs programmed into it. To do otherwise would cause confusion.

In adulthood, we add to our beliefs and sometimes change them. The consensus, however, pressures us to conform, to be *normal.* Being otherwise is being odd, unpredictable, and a threat to the status quo.

The reality we create is a product of our beliefs, but we misinterpret our reality as a validation of our beliefs. The consensus has taught us that *experience* creates belief. That truth is quite limiting. The opposite truth is liberating and powerful, for it allows us to change experience by changing beliefs.

To grow as human beings and as spiritual beings means mentally stepping outside of the constraints of the consensus's belief system.

There can be no growth without change and no positive change without dropping limiting beliefs and replacing them with more expansive ones.

That is part of the adventure of life and of spirituality.

RELIGION

Every establishment and convention of the modern world is a product of the masculine mind set which has prevailed since the rise of male chauvinism thousands of years ago. Organized religion is one of those establishments.

Under the influence of male chauvinism, religions developed which were solely the expression of male energy out of balance.

In many religions, God was created as a reflection of

the worst of human qualities—as domineering, judgmental, capricious, and cruel. He has been presented as a hateful and vindictive warrior who created women inferior to, and therefore subservient to men.

Some religions were established like paramilitary organizations with a hierarchical power structure ruled by a singular authority demanding dictatorial control over believers.

The God created by the world's major religions is to be feared—and loved out of fear. A difficult task indeed. So much is missing from those religions. Jesus, a metaphysician, was introduced into some of them to soften the message—and to act as a buffer against the wrath of God—but even his teachings of love and tolerance were distorted by those with agendas for control. The Golden Rule to treat others as we would have them treat us originated with pagan Goddess-worshipping religions. It was written into the New Testament and was meant to replace the rigid laws of the Old Testament's Ten Commandments, but that was not allowed to happen.

The religions created out of the male chauvinistic mind set were established to eradicate the Goddess and every trace of Her. All written references to Her were eliminated. Her temples and shrines were destroyed and upon their sites were erected churches and cathedrals to exalt the male-oriented God.

Women remained as reminders of Her feminine energy and they were devalued. And finally, the male-dominant religions devalued every aspect of femininity except for what they defined and allowed for the purpose of serving men. Religions became arid and sterile belief systems.

It is helpful to understand the connections between the global shift in consciousness, over the millennia, in favor of patriarchal societies and the simultaneous rise of male-dominant organized religions.

The early religions whose artifacts have been identified by archeologists, go back to at least 30,000 BC on what is now the European continent, and from 10,000 to 6,500 BC in certain other areas. Not all areas of the world have been explored by archeologists, but those which have, reveal that similar, nature loving, highly spiritual, artistic cultures once lived in harmony and peace with each other and with their environment. Artifacts from the remnants of those cultures indicate that they included worship of the Goddess and nature in their religions and that religion was a part of daily life.

In the most ancient times, in areas now Japan, India, Europe, North America, Siberia, China, and Tibet, there were small societies which had similar spiritual connections to the earth, the elements, the partnership of Goddess and God, birth, death, and regeneration.

Over the millennia, as the worldwide rise of masculine energy imbalance created a shift in consciousness, the ancient religions changed.

The following is a brief comparison of old and new forms of a few of the major religions:

EASTERN RELIGIONS

Shintoism

Shintoism, the religion native to Japan, goes back to prehistoric times. It originated from tribal religions which celebrated nature, including the elements, and recognized that everything was a living consciousness created by the devine god, Izanagi, and goddess, Isanami. By 500 AD, influenced by the organized religion of Buddhism and neighboring Chinese cultures, Shintoism too became more structured and shifted to the veneration of ancestors and the worship of certain deities, *kami*.

From 1867 to 1912, the Meiji period, Shinto became an aspect of patriotism and national ideology known as *State* Shinto. After Japan's defeat in World War II, the religion was decentralized and reformed into smaller sects as *Shrine* Shinto.

Today, the male head of each family clan is considered a priest. The Emperor, head of the imperial family, is the highest priest. Shintoism, almost exclusively practiced by those of Japanese descent, stresses moral values and respect for tradition, family and state. Modern Japanese society is male dominant and stresses loyalty to authority—state, employer, and family patriarch.

Hinduism

Hinduism, is a collection of beliefs and practices which were founded by the agrarian cultures residing in the regions now India and Asia. The various belief systems which are collectively Hinduism are based upon the *Sanatana Dharma*, dating back 10,000 years, as eternal truths expressed by great seers.

When patriarchal Aryan nomads invaded northern India during the 2nd millennium BC, their culture and religion became integrated with the local agrarian communities. Under the influence of rising male domination, certain Hindu beliefs were established as spiritual *law* in various writings. The Vedanta, the final text of the *Sanatana Dharma*, was written between 200 and 800 AD.

Over the millennia, the ancient beliefs in the equality between goddess and god, men and women, were superseded by beliefs in various male gods with female consorts. Likewise, in modern Hindu societies, women have been devalued except for their supportive role to men and their ability to bear their husband's sons.

Buddhism

The Buddha, or *enlightened one,* Siddhartha Guatama, was born a prince in Nepal near the border of India in the 6th Century BC. As a young man, he was troubled by the conditions of society in the region.

After studying various Hindu teachings in his adulthood and living in extreme austerity—with frequent fasting and extensive meditation—he abandoned established religious systems to seek his own spiritual enlightenment. He found it while meditating alone seated under a tree.

Following his enlightenment, he traveled far and wide over the next forty-five years preaching sermons to all who would listen. His teachings centered around four truths—the *fact* of universal suffering, the *cause* of suffering, the *overcoming* of suffering, and the *way* of overcoming suffering.

He presented the method of overcoming suffering as an eight-step path of right thinking and behavior to be followed by those seeking liberation—nirvana—from self-centered desires and attachments. Achieving nirvana is a slow process requiring self denial and numerous incarnations to work through the karma of previous lifetimes.

Belief in karmic law is inherent to Buddhism, which is practiced by about 500 million followers, mostly in Asian countries. The effect of Buddhism has been the control and pacification of masses of have-nots who might otherwise believe that they are entitled to freedom from suffering at any time they desire it.

WESTERN RELIGIONS

Ancient Mediterranean cultures were agrarian, matrilineal goddess-worshippers. As migrations of central European peoples, whose cultures had been changed by the invasions of patriarchal Kurgans[23] from southern Russia, infiltrated the Mediterranean area, those societies also began to change.

The upsurge in masculine energy in the Mediterranean area influenced the various religions in that region. At times, the Goddess was seen as the *highest* deity in the hierarchical religious systems which evolved from rising male chauvinism. Eventually, She was broken into the various aspects of Herself, given numerous names and worshipped accordingly. Although some would like to idealize the later goddess-worshipping religions, it was within them that the practice of blood sacrifice was utilized—first with animals, then with humans.

All of the world's most successful civilizations were created out of a partnership between men and women. An imbalance of masculine and feminine energies eventually brought about their destruction.

Women in the ancient Roman, Egyptian, Greek, and Etruscan societies attained distinctive levels of power, freedom, independence, and wealth. Many were healers and priestesses. Some of the pharaohs were women. In time, however, resentment of the powerful women grew. Male

chauvinism holds that only one authority can be in power—
"Either I'm in charge, or you are."[24]

The later goddess-worshipping religions eventually
reached the point where the emphasis on second Chakra
sexuality outweighed the expression of higher Chakra spirituality. With the over-emphasis on sexuality, powerful
priestesses willingly relinquished their authority to men,
who stepped into leadership as priests.

In rebellion against the power of women in society and
religion and to gain power for themselves, male leaders, at
different times in different areas, conspired to consolidate
the various local pagan religions into a singular, more powerful, male-oriented religion with written laws to be obeyed.
Organized religions were thus created to polarize societies.

Judaism

The mystical origins of Jewish religion were based upon the
equality of gods and goddesses and of men and women.
Elohim is the Hebrew word for the goddesses and gods.
According to legend, around 1300 BC, Moses, as leader of
the Israelites banished from Egypt, presented to his people
certain laws known as the Ten Commandments which he
claimed God had given him on top of a mountain.

The Commandments were similar to both the laws of
the Canaanite god Baal-Berith—God of the Convenant—
and the commandments of the Buddhist Decalogue. Such
laws from higher sources were most often given to the
recipient in a remote location with no one else present.

The Ten Commandments produced by Moses, and
other written texts including the Torah—the Old Testament Books of the Bible—formed the basis of Judaism, the

first organized religion. Judaism created a patriarchal God as singular authority and law-giver.

Judaism had the effect of unifying the Hebrew people under the leadership of Moses.

Christianity

Christian theology, or Christianity, is founded upon the teachings of Jesus Christ as presented in the Holy Bible, which is considered to be the word of God. Jesus lived from about 8-4 BC until around 27-30 AD. Changes to the calendar make the dates indefinite.

Around 100 AD, the first fragments of the New Testament appeared. They were about the life of Jesus, written after his death by no one who had personally known him. The earliest book of the New Testament was believed to have been written by Paul about 51 AD He had never seen Jesus, nor did he personally know details of his life. Over the ensuing centuries, details of Jesus' life were pieced together from the myths and legends of various early mystery schools and religions in Asia, India, the Middle East, the Mediterranean area, and Europe. Some Books of the New Testament were attributed to Jesus' actual apostles, though they were written by others much later.

The title of Christos—Anointed One—had been given to many Middle-Eastern sacrificial gods. Good Shepherd, King of Kings were titles of other elder gods. The mythology of Christianity produced many accounts of miracles, healings, and sayings attributed to Jesus, but traceable to a variety of ancient pagan religions and their gods. Some of the earlier religions had a Mother and Son who would, on occasion, evict Father from heaven. Jesus, as the son of God created by Christianity, was obedient and submissive to his Father-God.

By the 4th Century AD, in addition to the indigenous nature-religions, there were a multitude of Christian sects, each with its own set of Gospels. They were to be consolidated, over time, into a single powerful religion.

Constantine, a convert to Christianity, was the first Roman Emperor to legalize Christianity. The Roman Church was established in the eastern part of the Empire, beginning in 313 AD, by committees of men who held meetings to develop its official doctrines. All references to reincarnation were deleted from the tenets of the Church. The Virgin Mary was a token reference to the Goddess provided to appease new converts who would not totally abandon Her.

The Roman Empire consisted of most of the Mediterranean region and much of Europe. To create political unity and strength, the entire Roman Empire was officially converted to Christianity. It became the Holy Roman Empire.

In 1054 AD, with the decline of the Roman Empire, the Western faction of the Church split away from the Eastern Church. Roman Catholicism was established by the Latin western church as the one true Church. The word *catholic* means *universal.* The western church became the Roman Catholic Church.

The Middle Ages began with the organization of the Roman Catholic Church. That period designates the time during which the Church, in alliance with the State, instigated a series of bloody crusades over several hundreds of years to either subjugate foreign peoples through religious conversion or to slaughter the holdouts. In either case, those assaulted were divested of their lands and other wealth.

Though there are no records as evidence, it is estimated that the crusades, inquisitions, genocides, and similar activities carried out in the name of the Church caused the extermination of up to 14 million people, mostly women. The properties confiscated formed the basis of the tremendous wealth and power of the patriarchal Church. The Middle Ages are also known as the Dark Ages because the Church set about destroying every evidence of education, science, and religion not sanctioned by official Catholic doctrine.

Their power and wealth were expanded as Church and State began to explore and colonize the new world, beginning about 1500 AD.

In the early 17th Century, the printing press was invented in Germany and for the first time the Bible was widely available to those not a part of Church hierarchy.

There followed a proliferation of Christian religions established in protest against the supreme authority of the Catholic Church. Various versions of the Bible were written and rewritten, all produced from the prevailing male mind set.

Protestant religions spread and more native blood flowed as European émigrés infiltrated the New World, coercing indigenous folk, whose lands they were confiscating, to convert to western religion.

Islam

In the 6th Century AD, in a cave near the City of Mecca, a young man named Mohammed claimed to have been given the message of Islam by the angel Gabriel. He proclaimed that what was told to him confirmed what previous prophets of Judaism and Christianity had taught.

Once again, the pagan religions with their varieties of gods and goddesses, practiced by most people throughout the region, were denounced and Mohammed declared that there was only one true God, known in Islam as Allah.

Eventually, though not without bloodshed, Mohammed gathered a large following. Within ten years the entire Arabian Peninsula was converted to Islam, a generation later, a region the size of the United States was converted. In present times there are over a billion believers worldwide and Islam, the youngest of the major western religions, is one of the fastest growing organized religions.

The world's major western religions, each set forth as *the* authority of what is spiritual, have in common beliefs in a supreme male deity, the value of guilt and shame, rigid laws that dictate sexual conduct and procreation, and the suppression of self-determination and spiritual exploration.

All major religions promote the predominance of men over women.

II. Spirituality, the Goddess and True God

*W*e created religion in our reality to remind us that there *is* something more so we wouldn't have to rediscover that each lifetime. It is for us to find out for ourself what the *more* is. We get a start by either exploring or ignoring religion, but we must not stop there if we are to expand our spirituality.

Each of us in one lifetime or another turned away from the Goddess. We did so because we thought She had betrayed or abandoned us. We misunderstood the event that made us feel abandoned or betrayed. It was we who had created the reality, but we blamed Her instead. Our rejection of the Goddess may have happened at a time of personal crises when we called upon Her, in vain, to save us.

Humanity, too, turned its back on the Goddess, perhaps when She did not rescue it from the destruction of civilizations past.

The Goddess loves us too much to interfere in our growth, though She is always there to encourage it and to help when we ask Her to.

If we create realities out of faulty beliefs or from the

imbalance of masculine and feminine energies, it is for us to discover. It is for us to change.

The Goddess *is* returning—though it was never She who left. There are many of us now who sense at higher, unconscious levels of ourself, that She comes and we are panicked by Her return.

We fear that She is as vindictive as the God we created and worshipped. We feel shame and undeservability because we denounced Her, betrayed and abandoned Her in lifetimes past.

But She and the true God love unconditionally. They do not punish.

We need to come to terms with our fears about Her return. We need to forgive ourselves for turning away from Her. And we need to welcome Her back—each in our own way, in our own time.

She is there with Her arms open wide, awaiting our return. She is the Mother we have sought in every lifetime. She is the Mother who loves us no matter what we do. She is the Mother who knows we already *are* the spiritual beings who have transcended the lower realms. And She is much more.

She is the innocent Maiden full of hope and the Crone wise and kind. She is the powerful Woman. She is the Warrior who defends truth. She is the Lover who knows how to love and can teach us to as well. She is the totality of these energies, greater than the sum of the parts.

Through the Goddess, we will meet the true God.

He, the loving Father who provides and protects. He, with the wisdom of the Old Man and the curiosity of the Adventurer.

God and Goddess, together, form a synergy which is powerful and loving. That combination of power and love is available to each of us, to discover for ourself as we travel our spiritual path Home.

CHAPTER 6

Discovering Our Soul, Awakening Our Spirit

Discovering Our Soul,
Awakening Our Spirit

*O*ur Soul is our connection to the Goddess. It is an aspect of Her love. Our Spirit is an aspect of God's energy and love. Our link with the Goddess can be more firmly established as we open ourself to our Soul. We move toward Her as we meet and blend with our Soul. We will find and be embraced by our Soul as we learn to express our deepest feelings, as we learn to use our imagination fully and richly, as we learn to love ourself more and more. We will not do it perfectly, may not do it completely, but it will be enough.

Our Soul emanates from the womb of the Goddess and when it combines with the spark of God's thought that is our Spirit, it recreates our connection to Them. In that way, we establish ourself a spiritual being. That connection helps us consciously create all that *is* in our reality following the pattern established by Goddess and God in Their creation of All That Is. A minute portion of the hologram, in that way, contains a picture of it all.

Finding our Soul can lead us to our chosen focuses in this lifetime for they are our Soul's path. As we fulfill them, we follow that path.

Our Soul is an aspect of our Higher Self and as we

grow spiritually we three shall become one.

Throughout our lifetime, our Soul is there to tend to us. If we do not seek it out where it dwells in the unconscious world and the underworld—a sliver on the underside of our unconscious mind, it comes to us at critical times of our life.

Whenever we experience severe trauma, severe pain of any type, we lose a part of ourself. We leave a part of ourself behind. Because our Soul is dedicated to us and will never abandon us, a piece of It stays behind with the part we have lost. By healing the past through meditative means, we can gather and integrate those lost parts of ourself and our Soul.

There are certain times of initiation, times of passage from one phase to another throughout our life. Our soul is there to guide us, sometimes to slow us down or to accelerate our passage. Though we may neglect our Soul, it is with us always. It provides opportunities for growth, if only we would recognize them.

FACES OF OUR SOUL[25]

The Soul may enter our physical body at any time up to seventy-two hours after birth. If it has not by then, we do not remain physical.

Name

The name we are given at birth is the grounding of our Soul to the Physical Plane. Our name has a specific meaning related to our purpose in the new lifetime. Most often it has nothing to do with the reasons parents chose our name. The Name is the first face of our Soul.

Power

As children, beginning at about eighteen months, we move into the period where we discover our personal power. At first we learn that we are not a part of our mother but quite separate and that is when we begin to explore our world. We find freedom in our mobility and as we develop, we discover our own thoughts and feelings.

During this phase we need guidance from parents or other caregivers to define the principles, character, integrity, and ideals which will help us establish our self-esteem. Sadly, the guidance is often lacking.

The second face of our Soul appears during the Power phase. It comes to assist as aspects of child-energies emerge in pairs—the Naive One with its infant innocence always hopeful, always assuming it is loved, and the Waif—born out of the child's first feeling of rejection—who learns how to fend for itself. The Fighter who carves out and protects its space in the world and the Nurturer who loves and cares for itself and others. The Seeker of Truth who searches for life's meaning and the Seeker of Love who seeks love for itself.

All of the parts show themselves during the Power phase. One of the six will take the lead and the other five will subordinate, but under ideal conditions, they all become integrated and a happy, free child is produced.

Often, however, the traumas of childhood alter the positive side of the energies, or require that some be submerged in order for the child to survive mentally, emotionally, even physically.

When the Innocent or the Waif cannot remain, the Fighter or the Nurturer are all that are left.

Frequently the Fighter aspect is not allowed to be expressed in the child's environment and it is suppressed. Or if it is expressed, it is in a negative form—as bully. When *all* that is left above the line is the Fighter, many times that person becomes a criminal.

If only the Nurturer aspect is allowed in order to survive, the person becomes a martyr, always doing for and giving to others. The Nurturer/martyr learns to manipulate and control through nurturing.

The Seeker of Truth may be submerged or may lose its sense of self in its intellect—all thought, little feeling. The Seeker of Love is either submerged, resulting in denial of love, or is constantly searching for love from others.

The Soul aids in this process of survival, seeing to it that the aspects of the child not allowed to be expressed and integrated are not lost, but are submerged into the Shadow Self. Parts of the Soul stay behind to care for those aspects.

Eternal Youth

As the Power phase of childhood moves into adolescence, the next face of the Soul is revealed. It comes during that time, however brief—usually between thirteen and eighteen years of age, when the adolescent feels the most powerful, the most invincible. That period is called Eternal Youth and it marks the emergence of internal energies described as the Magician and the Master.

The Magician within can manifest anything through its personal power. The Master knows all of the answers, therefore can solve any problem. One of the two, either Magician or Master, is more predominant, the other subsidiary, during this period. The adolescent, for the first time alive with passion, experiences a flash of the magic and mastery that is available with conscious creation. They sense their power and immortality.

And then something happens. They fly too close to the flame.

Wounding

A trauma, a disappointment, perhaps a tragedy occurs which brings the adolescent down from the heights. That is the Wounding, a mortal blow that will change them.

Once again aspects of self, now Magician and Master, are either submerged into the shadows or the negative aspect of the predominant one is exposed. The Magician can become a dark force—evil, the Master, a tyrant.

It is at this time of Wounding when the fourth face of the Soul appears.

In ancient cultures the Wounding was understood as an opportunity for great learning about self, as a time that prepares the way for transition into adulthood. Wise ones would sit with the adolescent and talk with them about what had been experienced and the reasons for it. Growth through insight would occur.

In modern societies, the Wounding is a time for denial, for suppressed feelings, because failure and remorse are not allowed. It is a time for deepening the shame and undeservability felt early in childhood.

After the Wounding, in order to bring stability to the chaos, the adolescent must explain to themself through logic and reason the *why* of what happened. The Dark Law is created. It might be the Law that says When Everything is Going Right, Something Bad Happens. Or a Law that says I Can Never Have What I Really Want.

Like other beliefs formed in adolescence, the Dark Law is firmly established in the subconscious mind. Ever after, being the good servant, the subconscious mind delivers realities consistent with the Dark Law.

The Wounding lasts but a short while yet it profoundly impacts for a lifetime—unless uncovered and dealt with. Again, a piece of our Soul stays with that part of us lost in time as the wounded adolescent.

Shadow

As we move beyond the Wounding, we experience a new phase.

All of the aspects of ourself we have denied and suppressed—the emotions, the shame, our sense of deservability, our blockages and payoffs, the components of self from Waif to Magician—all of the elements we have not dealt with have been submerged into our unconscious mind. Submerged into our Shadow. We encounter the next face of our Soul as the Shadow Self. The Shadow period may last the rest of our life.

Two more energies of self also appear during the Shadow phase. They are the Creator and the Destroyer.

The Shadow period is a time to learn what lies within our Shadow Self from the realities we manifest. If we use the realities as feedback which lets us know what inner change is needed, what parts of our Shadow must be dealt with, and act upon that knowledge, we experience growth and the empowerment of consciously creating our reality.

Those aspects of self buried in our Shadow are presented to us in the form of people closest to us. The ones toward whom we feel the strongest emotions, from love to hatred, represent the parts of ourself which we have refused to look at or to even admit we have. To help us see them, our Soul pushes these others forward. Most often, they are family members and friends—or enemies.

World events about which we have the strongest feelings also are reflections of our Shadow Self. Our violent nature and our prejudice which we refuse to own and process. Our errant thoughts, which we judge as vile and disgusting, and quickly dismiss because we don't want to admit we have them. Our darkest secrets which we refuse to acknowledge to ourself. The clues to what we deny in ourself are played out upon the world stage. The fact that we react excessively to certain occurrences in our reality indicates their connection to our Shadow Self.

Often the most beautiful aspects of ourself also reside in our Shadow, for we have denied and suppressed them as well. Many of our strengths, talents, and gifts are hidden there. We create others near us who have those qualities we admire and envy to show us what we do not see in ourself.

Using brutal honesty, we can identify those aspects which we need to deal with in our subconscious and unconscious minds. With the help of the Destroyer energy, we can destroy all of what has been—that is, we can eliminate the *influence* of the past. Employing the Creator energy we can create new present realities and a new future.

Through our Shadow work, we learn how to consciously create success and to learn how to have fun by *engaging* reality, rather than escaping from it through alcohol, drugs, food, and other addictions. That is the fulfillment of two of our focuses.

With the help of our Soul, more and more we produce our reality from our Shadow Self to give ourself frequent opportunities to bring forth and respond to what is buried there. Our micro and macro worlds are the manifestation of what resides in our subconscious and unconscious minds. The more responsibility we assume, the more freedom and power we have to change them. There are meditative ways to discover and process what lies within before it is demonstrated in our physical world. (See Resources.)

Our Soul speaks to us through our imagination. If we cut ourself off from that communication, our Soul can only speak to us through crisis.

As we transform our dark Shadow to a light Shadow by examining what lies in the realm of our unconscious mind —dealing, not with *all* of it, but with the most significant and impactful parts—we can free ourself to imagine new realities. We can share our Soul's imagination and together create a different world.

Double

Beyond the Shadow phase, at around fifty years of age, we encounter the face of our Soul called the Double. It arrives at a time when we feel, at some level, a yearning to turn Homeward. Our Soul has two faces at the time of the Double. One looks backward, to times past. One looks forward to the future.

The Double signifies the choice we have at this time— to cling to the past, perhaps to return to it mentally and emotionally, or to look forward to the future with curiosity and enthusiasm. That choice is always with us, of course, but it is especially clear at this time of life.

Those who want to return to the past often develop mentally and emotionally disabling conditions. Often they become more and more childlike as they progress through old age, sometimes deteriorating into an infantile state. Or they develop physical ailments and die quickly in order to begin anew.

Others, who choose to detach emotionally from the past and to return Home by way of the future, may live very long lives. Instead of returning to childlike or adolescent behavior, they bring the freedom of the child and the curiosity of the adolescent with them into old age.

The Double is a time when great change can occur if the decision is made to let go of the past. Clinging to the past by anyone at any age retards growth. When we let go of it at this time of the Double, we open the way for rapid personal and spiritual growth—if there is also a choice to expand awareness and if decisions are made which take us in that direction.

During the time of the Double, two more components of the energies of self emerge. They are the Wise One and the Old Fool.

If the road traveled is the one leading to the future and if self-knowledge is acquired along the way, the traveler becomes the Wise One. Wise, not from age itself, but from a never-ending expansion of awareness and accumulation of self-knowledge. Understanding is awareness put into action. Wisdom is *living* our understanding.

If the road backward to times past has been chosen, rather than the Wise One, its negative aspect, the Wiseacre, comes forth. The Wiseacre expresses adolescent know-it-all, black or white absolutes, stubbornly refusing to learn anything new. Lacking true wisdom, they rely on platitudes and clichés.

In advanced old age, we become either a happy Old Fool or a silly Old Fool. The term "fool" is not derogatory in this sense. It designates the time when there are no problems, the time of being care-free. The happy Old Fool has no problems for that is the reality they created out of wisdom. Longevity of mind, body, and spirit is produced from joy and wisdom.

The silly Old Fool has no problems because they have mentally retreated from the physical world.

Parts of our Soul again stay behind when we opt for Wiseacre or silly Old Fool.

Remains

The last face of our Soul is that of the Remains. It comes to us when we near death's threshold to ease our birth into the next world, as it did when we entered this one.

When we reach this passage, at the time of our death, we have the opportunity to consciously lift our energy—our ethereal body—out of our physical body, providing we have attained that level of awareness and responsibility. With it, we can *consciously* choose the time and place of our death. We do so when we feel we have completed what we wanted to do in the lifetime. We are not afraid of death for we know it is only a death of the physical body and the transcendence of our eternal consciousness beyond physical limitations.

The elegance of this type of passage is quite different from how most of us experience dying and death. We are frightened by it and do everything to stay physically alive because we fear what is unknown. Even with religious beliefs about life after death and heaven, to most death is a fearsome prospect.

It is through the empowerment of consciously taking responsibility for creating one's physical life that the empowerment for gracefully leaving it arises.

The seven faces of our Soul are shown to us through the phases of our life. Each phase is an opportunity to embrace our Soul and become one with it. If we recognize that the phases are *spiritual* experiences, that they have *spiritual* significance for us, then we may open to our Soul and can be uplifted by the experience. Using meditative techniques, we can go back to re-experience any phase and to heal *that* self as the aware adult we now are. We can return to past woundings and crises to collect the parts of self left behind—perhaps the Fighter or the Innocent—so that we can integrate all components to form a functioning whole.

We can be transformed by any experience if we recognize the negative aspects of ourself which produced the reality, understand the payoffs we got from it, forgive ourself for creating the reality, and then make the necessary changes within.

We can become one with our Soul by experiencing our emotions fully and deeply. By allowing our imagination to come alive with passion and compassion and reason and logic. By utilizing our intuition and the feedback our body gives us. By seeking beauty and harmony in our surroundings, for those are the things loved by our Soul.

ASPECTS OF OUR SPIRIT

Our Spirit resides within our Mind. It is a spark of thought from God's mind. Intellect, logic, and reason comprise but a portion of what is contained as the Spirit within our Mind. Spirit is also our *aliveness.*

There are some whose Spirit has been extinguished and must first be resurrected in order for them to fully participate in life. But for many, the spark that is Spirit lies dormant from lack of stimulation. We accept the status quo of the consensus mind set and it has a narcotic affect on our thinking process. That is one of the ways we give our power away.

To awaken the sleeping Spirit, we must take our power back. We can do this by developing self-trust and by developing our skills of judgment—not to judge the value of others, but to judge their value as a *source of information*.

We must also develop our ability to form opinions and to make growth choices and decisions. We do this by weighing information we have gathered and relying as well on the inner feelings we have—our gut feelings and our intuition. In that way we are listening to what our physical body tells us and also what our psychic body is saying.

If we rely on these inner voices and combine that reliance with the logic and reason of our intellect, we can create a solid foundation for self-trust.

Self-trust is a focus many have in life—learning to establish it and then with it, learning to trust selected others.

The more self-trust we have, the less likelihood there is of becoming a victim. There is a time for innocence—as we approach new opportunities with the freshness and optimism of a child. But we must also engage our sense of judgment and self-trust, forming opinions and making choices based on them as an adult.

The Spirit, once energized in this way becomes a self-generator of thoughts and ideas. Thoughts and ideas become a part of the creative process and we then bring in our feelings. We listen to what they say to us. In that way creativity is born.

Creativity is consciously conceiving anything that is new. Productivity is learning something new about ourself from what we have created. All of reality is an opportunity for creativity and productivity.

The Spirit is the engine that keeps us running in the sense that consciousness is what we are.

The stimulation of Spirit increases our *aliveness.* The aliveness that creates enthusiasm—for life. Very old people who have that Spirit, that spark of aliveness, seem far younger than their years. It is quite apparent. It is a light that shines from within.

One of the keys to longevity is to light that spark and to keep it burning.

Curiosity is another aspect of Spirit. The more we have of it, the more opportunities we create to explore. If we find within our adult self the curiosity of the adolescent and combine it with our courage and self-confidence—with those assets life *is* an adventure. It is not necessary to travel to distant lands to find it. We can explore the reality we've created as our personal life. For many it is unknown territory.

Life becomes the exciting journey it was meant to be. Exploring life as we create and re-create it becomes the fun we continually learn to have at each stage along the way. With Spirit and Soul combined there is a richness and depth to life quite lacking without them.

We are an intricate collection of fluid energies which are woven together in an unsteady pattern. There is no single solution, no single method for living life or for growth. We must find our own pattern, our own resonance.

When we find and embrace our Soul and activate our Spirit, we lift our resonance in the universe to a higher vibrational frequency.

At that higher frequency, we attract and are attracted to like frequencies. We will be aware of the lower vibrations—the different reality—but we will be at home in a reality created by those who resonate in a unique harmony. There will be fewer problems and less pain. Eventually, we could create a reality with no problems and no pain. Only we set the limitations.

CHAPTER 7

Unseen Realms and Unseen Friends

Unseen Realms and Unseen Friends

*T*here are realms of reality beyond our illusion which we cannot see with our physical eyes. Some co-exist with us on our Physical Plane at the same time but within a different space. Other realms share our space, but at times we would call past or future. In the hologram of our illusion, these multiple realities are possible, though difficult to comprehend in a consensus mind-set.

Mineral, plant, and animal kingdoms exist in our same space and time, yet the conscious levels of those realms— the consciousness energies which are a part of them—have been obscured to our senses by the consensus belief systems which have evolved over thousands of years.

When we moved from having dominion in our environment into seeking domination over it, we severed our connections to those other realms, so alive with conscious energy.

There was a time when humankind was aware of the community of nature. There are so-called "primitive" people today who still have that awareness.

The difference between those primitives and ourself is merely belief, for primitive people create their reality just as we each do, out of beliefs and the attitudes, thoughts, feelings, choices, and decisions which flow from them.

The conscious energies which fill the other realms of our physical domain are evolving consciousnesses which have much to offer as co-creators, if only we would expand our awareness enough for mutual communication. We have legends and lore about fairies, elves, gnomes, leprechauns, genies, unicorns, and such other entities created with imagination out of belief—like all our illusion. The physical characteristics of the imaginary folk are produced solely by the belief of the one who perceives them. Their existence as downstepped energies who reside in their respective kingdoms cannot be scientifically proven—just as the realness of solid matter cannot—but that doesn't mean they don't exist.

The plant realm consciousnesses are known as "devas." Each plant, no matter its size or tenure on earth, has a deva. Likewise, minerals and animals have conscious spirit-souls with thoughtful intelligence and emotional feeling. Each has spiritual worth equal to our own.

Children are more open to the other realities. They often know their unseen friends. As children grow, they become more and more influenced by the limited beliefs of the consensus world and the part of their imagination that opened them to the other realms begins to fade and finally vanishes.

The elements of nature—air, water, fire, and earth—are powerful forces but without intelligence or feeling for they are not conscious energies. Yet, by allowing ourself to personify each in meditation, it is possible to work with those energies for mutual benefit. The personifications are metaphysical archetypes known through the ages as Raphael (air), Michael (fire), Gabriel (water), and Ariel (earth).

The elements are components in the grand scheme of nature—birth, growth, death, and regeneration—which symbolizes the pattern of our spirituality. In areas where winter weather does not kill vegetation, hurricanes, fires, landslides, tidalwaves occur. They clear away what was, to make way for what will be. As we willingly do the same in our own life, the metaphor will not play out so harshly in nature.

All of the universe works in harmonious co-operation except for humankind. We can re-establish our connection to that harmony by acknowledging and respecting the energies and forces with which we share our home. We can learn to co-create with them.

Planet Earth, like all else at the physical level, is a hologram. It too has a living, highly evolved spirit-soul consciousness, referred to by some as "Gaia." Around the world, at various locations, are ethereal power centers of electro-magnetic energy—perhaps the Earth's Chakra centers. The ancients who were sensitive to such fields of energy marked many of them with standing stones and temples.

If lines were drawn to connect the primary centers of energy, we would see large ovals circling the planet, linked together in the Pacific Ocean by the energy of Lemuria and in the Atlantic by the energy of Atlantis.

The Earth's electro-magnetic energy fields *create* weather conditions, earthquakes, and other tectonic activity and EM energy is also *produced by* the storms and tectonic activity. Electro-magnetic energy fields are also created by topographical conditions around the world.

Expanses of still water and flat land, such as lakes, ponds, fields, and deserts, create a surface upon which the swirling energy collects and builds to form a vortex of energy. Areas where the winds blow strongly also create vortices of EM energy.

The sun in our solar system is, itself, a vortex of energy

(connected to the vortex of Sirius) which gives off electro-magnetic energy—more than its size should afford, according to scientific calculations—which directly impacts energy fields on our planet.

Electro-magnetic energy is one of the forces that exist between the realms. There is an increased level of electro-magnetic energy being generated at this time for a grand evolution that is taking place. (See Chapter 10.)

ASTRAL PLANE

Beyond our Physical Plane lies the Astral Plane where our consciousness goes to dream while our body is asleep. The Astral Plane resembles the Physical Plane except that it has the *concept* of time and space and within dreams, unlike our awake time, shifts in time and space can occur. On the Astral Plane, there exists the full array of human emotions. Our dreams are an indication of what lies submerged in our subconscious and unconscious minds. Much of the clutter gets expressed in dreams.

Dreams also are coded messages from our Higher Self about our strengths and what we need to process which has otherwise been ignored. If we experience strong emotions in our dream state, it is a clear message about emotions we have not consciously recognized, felt, and released, but which are influencing our reality.

All probable reality is created either on the Physical Plane or on the Astral Plane, including the best and the worst of it. If we learn about ourself from our dreams, we need not manifest the worst in our physicality.

The Astral Plane, like the Physical, resonates with many vibrational frequencies. People who pass from the Physical

Plane with the same limitations to growth that they had while physical will continue to create their reality from them, remaining close, in vibrational frequency, to the Physical Plane.

CAUSAL PLANE

The Causal Plane is a beautiful landscape of pastel-colored hills and meadows, at first appearing composed of geometric shapes but melding into a more familiar look as our senses adjust. There is but memory of hurt and pain there.

All that is possible, all of the causes and effects that we could imagine, exists on the Causal Plane. A belief is a vibrational frequency of possibility. The stronger our belief, the more likely that possibility will become probability, and probability a manifestation in our physical reality. When *our* possibilities overlay the possibilities which exist on the Causal Plane, they fall to the Astral Plane as probabilities.

By transporting the focus of our mind to the Causal Plane in meditation, in other words, by imagining ourself there, and then programming the reality we want to create, we can accelerate the actualization of that reality into physicality.

MENTAL PLANE

When we, as a consciousness, reach a certain level of awareness we can decide that we have learned as much as we need to through physical incarnation, and can choose to move on to a higher realm. Depending upon our particular belief system, the higher level may be the Mental Plane.

The Mental Plane is the highest (a word used here not for accuracy, for it is not accurate, but for facility) of the four lower levels we have created.

It, like the others, is manifested from belief. The emotions of hurt and pain do not exist there. It is the level known as "heaven" and depending upon one's concept of heaven, or lack thereof, the manifestation of the Mental Plane will conform accordingly. There are no sharp angles or points there, only soft curves.

Those of us who hold a belief in heaven will eventually find ourself in our own version of it on the Mental Plane with all the trappings there we expect—angels, harps and halos, streets of gold, puffy white clouds; an exclusive membership open only to those of similar belief.

We will remain on the Mental Plane in *our* heaven, believing we have reached the epitome of growth, perhaps for the equivalent of eons of time, until eventually we sense that there has to be something *more*—just as once we did in a human animal state on the Physical Plane. With that glimmer of light, away will fall the trappings of our heaven, and once again we will embark upon our journey of discovery, our journey Home.

There are infinite degrees of expanded awareness, for growth is exponential in all directions and we do not lose or leave behind what we were, we become *more* than we were by elevating our conscious attention.

If we hold beliefs in better-than/less-than hierarchical levels of growth and hierarchies of spiritual mastery, those beliefs, once again, are an expression of the masculine energy aspect of spirituality which seeks form and structure. Our spiritual *growth*, the expression of feminine energy, will always take us beyond such limitations when we are willing to give up our belief in them.

There are expanded levels of awareness beyond the lower planes where communication between entities occurs through an orgasmic blending of energy, a blending in which understanding of the other is instantly attained.

UNSEEN FRIENDS

We, in our human conceit, may believe that all conscious beings have chosen to be physical, but in actuality, most have not.

A relatively minute few of the infinite numbers of consciousness entities have ever chosen to be physical. Learning, growing, expanding occurs at limitless dimensions of awareness and will never be completed for God/Goddess/All That Is are forever expanding exponentially as They seek to become more of who They are.

We physical beings each have many unseen friends— friends from other realms, other levels of conscious energy —who not only know us by name, but who are dedicated to helping us, if only we would allow them to. Those friends are available to help us in our quest for spiritual growth. All we need do is be open to communication with them. What prevents us from doing so is our threshold of belief.

That threshold is quite high for some. It comes from the consensus belief system that says only that which can be physically touched, smelled, heard, and seen is real. It is necessary for us to step outside of the consensus mind set if we are to expand our awareness of other realms and unseen friends.

Our many unseen friends can be contacted in meditation or in the "blending" of our energies. On the Physical

Plane, we make friends by mutual attraction. It is our particular vibrational frequency and theirs which creates the connection. In the same way, unseen friends are attracted to us and we to them by vibrational resonance.

Beliefs we hold set the tone, so to speak, for our vibrational frequency and will impact our resonance. Those unseen friends who are attracted to us enough to communicate are coming from belief systems compatible with our own.

Many religions are based upon early communications from "angels" or other unseen beings who delivered "devine" guidelines for behavior to earthlings of compatible and receptive belief systems. Compatible resonance is the link between messenger and receiver of messages.

The origin of those messages most often was attributed to God—by the human recipient—but the true God does not interfere in our learning experience here on this planetary schoolground and, further, the magnitude of His energy is so great it could not be accommodated within the vibrational frequency of our universe.

Belief systems, no matter the origin, are always ultimately limiting and are meant to eventually be outgrown.

As we reach for the highest truth—the one with the least limitations—we attract those unseen friends who also subscribe to the higher and higher truths. The wisdom and awarenesses they can share with us are of great benefit to our personal and spiritual growth. Those with heightened awareness will not give us rules and orders to live by or to command others to adopt. Those unseen friends respect us and honor our dignity and value as human beings. At our request, they will offer suggestions and insights that can help us work through obstacles or create successes in our own life, but they will not do it for us nor take care of us, for that would rob us of our chance to learn how for ourself.

It is quite possible to establish communication with an unseen friend, an entity who may or may not have ever been physical. The Resources section offers references to help for doing so.

Most important, though, is to establish a communication and a rapport with our Higher Self, to open to their love and assistance, and to call upon them to help us be receptive to only those others who come to us in unconditional love. In that way we honor our own value and protect ourself from other entities who have more limited awareness and perhaps less regard for our human value. There are entities who are up to mischief, or worse, and will deliberately mislead us if we allow the negative aspects of ourself to be receptive to them.

It is our responsibility to protect ourself and to use discernment in evaluating the information we get from any source—on the Physical Plane and beyond—and we have our Higher Self to help us.

Being aware that there are other realms of conscious existence and knowing we have unseen friends who love us and want to help us succeed is an integral part of our spiritual growth.

CHAPTER 8

Clearing the Way for Growth

Clearing the Way for Growth

*T*he purpose of this chapter is to further identify the issues and obstacles with which we clutter our path of personal and spiritual growth. Sources of help for dealing with the issues and removing the obstacles are listed in the Resources section at the back of this book.

Clearing the path for personal and spiritual growth is an ongoing process which becomes easier with practice. The clearing will not be completed in a lifetime, for that is what life is about, but our expertise in dealing with them will allow us to sail over hurdles we used to crash into.

Finding the obstacles is the first step in the clearing process. It *is* a process and the *way* we do it is most important. It is the method and means of our spiritual growth. Some methods are more elegant, more efficient, than others.

Many people use struggle, hardship, pain, and suffering as a way to *earn* the right to grow. Those approaches may eventually work, but they are long and arduous. Many lifetimes must be devoted to growth through that kind of processing.

The more direct route, though it means sacrifice of a different kind, is through honestly recognizing the blockages that we have set up for ourself and taking responsibility for having put them there in the first place. Sacrifice enters into it when we realize we must give up the payoffs we enjoy by keeping the obstacles in place.

At birth, we bring into our new lifetime certain conditions, beliefs, and emotions which we've chosen as issues to focus on to further our growth. During infancy and childhood, our original issues are altered and added to. What evolves is a set of four boundaries which define the unique human being that we are. The boundaries are categorized as our *beliefs and image*, our *obstacles*—-the hurdles that we've chosen to overcome, our *contracts* with significant others *and scripts*—old life scripts to be rewritten, and our *brain chemistry and mechanics.*[26]

Our boundaries are the limitations to growth we have chosen to deal with in our lifetime. Dealing with these limitations means consciously exploring and expanding them, transforming and transcending them.

Our initial boundaries are changed in infancy, childhood, and adolescence by the impact of outside influences —primarily our relationships with our parents and others close to us. When we reach adulthood, we have the opportunity to examine our personal reality and to consciously make the changes necessary to improve it.

BELIEFS AND IMAGE

Beliefs

Beliefs and belief systems are discussed in Chapter 5.

Image

Personal image, like a bed of flowers and weeds, contains the *multiplicity of our identities*—growing in the garden of *our self-esteem.* Image is also *the impact produced by the synergy of those identities and self-esteem.* Self image is an integral part of our success or the lack of it. Like a garden, it is bountiful in some places and fallow in others.

Many of us create a new success in some area—money, career, recognition, a loving relationship—but because our self image cannot support the success, we sabotage it by losing what was gained or by undermining another part of our life. Our image must at least keep up with the success we've created in order to retain it.

To create and hold onto a particular future success, we need to expand beforehand our image related to it. It's important to dismantle the old image and replace it with a new one. One way that can be done is by writing out in free-flowing thoughts and words our present negative self image as it applies to our desired goal, including the belief we must currently hold to support it. Then, we write out a positive new image of the winner we want to become who has already achieved the success. After that, we choose a belief that winner would have in order to create the success.

In meditation, we instruct our subconscious mind to release the old limiting belief and to replace it with the new positive belief. Next we consciously release the old image, with much feeling and intent. (After the meditation, we tear up and dispose of the old image description.) Finally, we imagine and sense our new image as a shimmering robe of golden light which we happily slip into and gratefully wear.

To maintain our new image, we can remind our subconscious mind of it by putting small slips of paper of a special color, bearing our new belief, in places we will notice throughout the day.

OBSTACLES

Clinging to the Past

Clinging emotionally to the past hampers growth yet we continue to do it because we get the payoff of blaming others—most often those people and circumstances which have influenced our life as we have grown from infancy to the present.

As children, most of us were wronged in some way, some less overtly than others but just as impactfully. Whatever happened negatively influenced how we felt about ourself then and how we feel now. It is our responsibility as an adult to heal the wounded inner child and adolescent so their past hurts, angers, pains, or fears no longer influence our present life—and to end their negative impact on those close to us now.

With every problem we have three choices—to maintain the status quo, to blame others and wait for them to change, or to take responsibility and change ourself. Opting for the second solution can waste a lifetime.

We often blame our present circumstance on outside forces so that we can sit stubbornly in place and wait for the "other" to change, all the while feeling the victim, the martyr, perhaps stewing in righteous anger.

Blame is an easy obstacle to deal with. We simply stop doing it. However, because it has been habituated, ending blame takes practice. By paying close attention to our thoughts and feelings and when the urge to blame arises, by not doing so but assuming personal responsibility instead—we can drop the habit.

Projection and identification are other ways of clinging to the past—projecting mother or father onto certain oth-

ers or identifying ourself as parent or child in our relationships. We often project parent onto others in our current
reality to try to fix what went wrong in our childhood. To
create a happy ending to childhood misery. Or we identify
ourself as parent and project child onto others to manipulate, control, or punish as a way of acting out what we
endured as children.

The past has no power unless we empower it, has no
influence unless we allow it.

Many of us live our grown-up life as a failure in order
to punish our parents or to show the world what our parents did to us. That is another way of letting the past control us. Letting go of those negative motivations, creating
positive motivations instead, and always taking responsibility for the present will cut us loose from the past.

Self-Pity

Self-pity is the anesthetic we used as children to ease the
pain of our emotional wounds. It was necessary then for
our survival, but we got addicted to it and carried it with us
into our grown-up world. As a grown-up, however, we
soon learn that overt self-pity is distasteful to others, so we
modify it to victimhood or martyrhood.

Everything happens to a victim, they are responsible for
nothing. Victims have favorite arenas for demonstrating
their victimhood—relationships, health, finances, or work,
for instance. Lifelong victims are forever being taken advan-
tage of, are always being wronged or getting hurt. They are
victims of the world.

Martyrhood is a more sophisticated strain of self-pity.
The consensus tells us that selflessness, stoicism, and self-

deprivation somehow makes us a better person. Religions teach Sacrifice Now for Future Reward. Promoting such beliefs is a way to control and pacify the masses. But martyrhood, like other blockages, hinders personal and spiritual growth. There are ways of demonstrating love and of serving others without being a martyr.

Martyrs have hidden agendas. As martyrs, we punish those closest to us with our sighs, our phony sweetness (thinly disguising hostility), with our guilt-producing self-sacrifice, and in other unsubtle ways.

There are clues to help identify when we are in martyr. If we feel misunderstood, unappreciated, helpless and hopeless because we are burdened with burdens too heavy to bear, saddled with problems too difficult to solve, blamed for things we didn't do, and are punished for things not our fault [27]—we are being a martyr. Any one of those perceptions qualifies us.

Fear

Fear is an obstacle which can freeze us in place. It keeps us from making choices and from changing. It separates us from ourself and from our reality. We are no longer in charge of our destiny when we are fearful. It also keeps the past alive by motivating us to continually try fixing it through projection and identification. Fear is addictive and we use it to manipulate others. We use it as an excuse to justify our behavior. Fear separates us from our spirituality.

Fear has a positive side too. It is a warning that something is wrong and it tells us where we lack trust. For those reasons, we don't want to end fear, only conquer it. The way to do that is to openly admit our fear and to let ourself express the full emotion of it. Then we need to uncover and replace the underlying belief which has created the fearsome situation—actual or imagined.

Lack of Self-Trust

Everyone needs self-trust in order to grow personally and spiritually. Without it, we either have difficulty making decisions or we make them impulsively, with disastrous results. We can't determine who else is worthy of our trust and we are confused by choices. After learning to trust ourself, then —with discernment—we can trust selected others. Skepticism is healthy when we encounter the unknown. We use it as protection until we've assessed reliability. Without self-trust, however, healthy skepticism atrophies into stubborn cynicism.

Trust is produced by a synergy of our *rational thought, intuition, emotion,* and *body reaction.*[28] Most everyone is born with the potential for developing these capabilities, but their development is usually stunted or twisted on the way to adulthood.

Intuition is ridiculed *(women* have intuition), emotions are suppressed, the reactions of our body—physical health —are not recognized as being related to the non-physical, and rational thought is often distorted by the negative aspects of ourself.

We hear a number of voices in our head giving us guidance and it is confusing.

One of the voices is that of the inner critical parent, forever admonishing, berating, and frightening us. The critical parent is an amalgam of all the authority figures we've encountered—parents, teachers, religious leaders, and other *experts* on correct behavior. It uses guilt, fear, and self-punishment to maintain control. The critical parent is different from the inner nurturing parent which gives us positive parenting and protection.

Another voice is that of our negative ego.[29] It gets to each of us in the area where we are particularly vulnerable —perhaps being judgmental of others or righteously angry, or by blaming. It tells us that we are special. It is arrogant and self-important. Our negative ego wants us to be a victim and not responsible for our reality.

It is important that we understand the negative ego, for we all have one—and it is out to destroy us.

Just as animals are born with instinct to help them survive, humans are born with an ego. Our ego was meant only to deliver messages, which we were then supposed to consciously respond to, using our own discretion. But we became careless and lazy. We gave the responsibility for responding to the messages also to our ego. The ego is not equipped to discern, so it reacts automatically with whatever negative thoughts and feelings might be stored in our subconscious mind. That is when it becomes the *negative* ego.

An example of how the negative ego works is this: You loan your new car to your brother who must go for a job interview. When he returns the car, it has a dented fender. With a positive ego, the mental message delivered would simply be, "The fender is dented." The emotional response might be anger, concern over injuries, or other honest feelings. With the negative ego's input the message becomes, "My good-for-nothing brother has done it again. He's always been careless with my things. I know he's jealous of my success."

Because it lacks the capacity to cope with situations, the negative ego is angry for being made responsible, but contrarily it enjoys the power. Empowering our negative ego is like making a part time busboy the president of a chain of restaurants. After he's gotten over the glory of a plush office and a big salary, he realizes he's in over his head and he gets angry—but he doesn't want to relinquish the position.

Our negative ego is so angry it wants to destroy us. It has brought down many from the loftiest heights of success. A number of the famous and powerful have made unimaginable blunders which have ruined their lives. Though such ruination has been blamed on outside forces, including "the Devil," honest introspection would reveal a rampant negative ego.

In all cases, the negative ego has no power unless we allow it to participate in our reality. To end that, when it whispers to us in our thoughts, we just mentally say, "NO!" and refuse to let it interfere.

We also hear the voice of our wounded inner child who automatically reacts to situations familiar to its childhood experiences in order to relive old betrayals, rejections, abandonments, and other hurts in a vain attempt to undo them. The wounded adolescent's voice is there with its black or white judgments, with its prejudices and bigotry, with its rebellion and stubbornness.

To learn to trust ourself, we need to recognize these voices with their damaging messages and to refuse them.

We all have within us an inner voice that does have our best interest at heart. It is the voice of our intuition and conscience—our Higher Self. If we dismiss the other voices and allow ourself to listen to this quieter inner voice, using rational thought, paying attention to what our emotions and our bodies are telling us—we will develop self-trust.

We can begin to handle each of our blockages by first being honest enough with ourself to recognize them.

CONTRACTS AND SCRIPTS

Contracts

During our childhood, from about ages six to eight years, and later from about ages ten to twelve years, we either submit to or we establish personal emotional contracts with our parents as a mechanism to absorb the pain from the waves of shame which come at these times (see Chapter Nine). As adults we can identify and end the negative contracts which keep us tethered to the past.

Cloning contracts are a category of shame-based contracts made by the child to end the pain caused by the perfectionist or over-achieving parent who demands that their child be as good as they think *they* are. I will never make a mistake. I will be perfect. I will never be wrong. I will make you proud. I will be your product to show the world what a perfect parent you are. These are cloning contracts.

Cloning contracts are also made with violent, abusive, subhuman parents. I will become abusive too, to justify your abuse. I'll become a punisher of others or myself. I will never hurt/upset/anger you—or anyone else. I will become totally defensive—never admit I am wrong.

Another category of shame-based contracts are *opposing* contracts also made to stop the pain caused by superhuman or subhuman parents. I will never let you off the hook for what you have done to me. I'll become a failure/be sickly/always be unhappy to show the world how terrible you were.

Children make contracts with God in order to survive childhood. God, If you'll just get me through this (or give me) I promise I will always...

Contracts are also made between child and parent

around abandonment. I will never grow up. I will always be your baby. I will always seek your approval/advice/acceptance/praise/forgiveness. I will turn out the way you expect me to (as a failure or success). I will never leave you. I will become an extension of you. I will never be more successful/happier than you.

Familial contracts are linked to scripts played out in childhood.

If we have a psychic agreement with someone, our reality demonstrates it.

Scripts

We create our reality by either causing it or allowing it. As part of that creation process, we subconsciously write scripts for particular situations such as relationships, finances, work, and—in psychic co-operation—we find people agreeable to reading our lines. They too have a script with lines for us to read.

Often there are family dramas wherein each member, in silent co-operation, agrees to play a particular role—leader, black sheep, easygoing, victim, parent's favorite, martyr. Such scripted relationships can be uncovered by analyzing our interaction with family members and by recalling words and phrases we heard in childhood which give us clues.

The kinds of phrases which indicate a family script sound like these: No one will ever love you as much as your mother. I'll die if you ever leave me. Everybody picks on me. You're following in your brother's footsteps. She's the pretty one, her sister's the smart one. You're just like your father.

Out of family scripts, come contracts with family members.

If our script, written in childhood, has a role for someone willing to abuse us so that we can continue to be a victim, we will attract just the right one to play that part. In a room of five hundred people, the two with compatible scripts, ready to accommodate each other's needs—positive or negative—attract each other like iron to a magnet. Often it's called love at first sight.

Finding in our current reality, a situation similar to past experience will indicate where we've probably written a script. Negative scripts can be destroyed or re-written.

BRAIN CHEMISTRY AND MECHANICS

We human beings, unlike most animals, are born before our brain and nervous system are fully developed. That is why infants and young children need to sleep a great deal. Their brains and nervous systems continue to develop only when they sleep, and it is in the infant's and child's dream-sleep when the development occurs.

A number of things can happen during the brain/nervous system development stage which inhibit proper maturation. To understand what can go wrong, we need to understand some of the basics of our brain's composition and workings.

Our brain functions through electro-chemical and electro-mechanical interaction between its various parts, which include the reticular, limbic, and cerebral cortex portions. In a way, our brain is to our body's nervous system what a conductor is to a symphony orchestra.

The reticular portion is our oldest, most primitive brain and it regulates the autonomic nervous system—that part of the nervous system which controls the heart, muscle response, glands, and digestion. It also controls the release of adrenaline and chemicals active in the transmission of nerve impulse. It governs our physical survival through its regulation of our automatic bodily functions and through our involuntary "fight or flight" reactions.

The limbic portion of the brain is right next to the reticular brain. It is composed of a group of structures—including the hypothalamus and hippocampus—concerned with emotion and motivation. The limbic portion has to do with our emotional survival.

The cerebral cortex is the surface layer of gray matter covering the cerebrum (the newest portion of the brain) which functions chiefly in the coordination of higher nervous activity. It is the thinking/intellect part of the brain.

With healthy development of the brain's organic, chemical, and mechanical aspects, the individual sections of the brain interact through electro-magnetic impulses called *synapses*. That interaction produces a coordination of thoughts, feelings, and instinct. If our brain organ doesn't develop normally, if its chemistry is distorted, or if its mechanics become twisted, then our raw materials (beliefs, attitudes, feelings, thoughts, choices, and decisions) and our tools (imagination, desire, and expectancy) for reality creation are negatively affected.

To illustrate how the brain's development can be hampered in childhood by emotional trauma, Dr. Bernie S. Siegel writes, in *Love, Medicine & Miracles*:

"Nerve fibers enter the hypothalamus from nearly all other regions of the brain, so that intellectual and emotional processes occurring elsewhere in the brain affect the body. For example (in 1981), child-development researchers discovered 'psychosocial dwarfism,' a disturbingly common

syndrome in which an unhealthy emotional atmosphere at
home stunts a child's physical growth. When a child is
caught in a crossfire of hostility and feels rejected by his or
her parents, thereby growing up with little self-esteem, the
brain's emotional center, or the limbic system, acts upon
the nearby hypothalamus to shut off the pituitary gland's
production of growth hormones."

Chemical imbalance also causes more subtle, though
equally devastating damage. It diminishes the desire which
feeds our dreams for the future. Desire dwindles to hopes
and wishes and our dreams wither and die. Twisted mechanics pollute our raw materials and eliminate our tools for
manifesting what we want.

Errant brain chemistry and mechanics is caused in a
number of ways.

Some of us are born with those conditions because of a
pre-birth choice we made. For example, because we
believed in karma, perhaps we chose to deal with a particular issue in this lifetime—say, personal power—by eliminat-
ing (through altering our brain chemistry or mechanics) the
ability to recreate a past-life experience of misusing power.
Or we may have chosen to knock ourself out of phase for
the opportunity of consciously taking responsibility for cor-
recting the distortion. As a conscious being planning our
new lifetime, we chose to twist the mechanism.

Often it is a brain function disorder which short-circuits
the nervous system and creates a malfunction. Such a disorder is caused after birth in several ways. Infants need to be
lovingly touched and talked to. If they do not receive
enough of that nurturing attention, their abilities to think
and feel are inhibited. If children are not allowed to express
their feelings, not allowed to think, if they do not have
enough laughter and imaginative play in their lives, devel-

opment of their brain and nervous system is thwarted. When children or infants suffer life-threatening abuse or if they experience great physical or emotional trauma—such as premature birth or witnessing the death of a parent—brain chemistry and mechanics are altered.

Shame which has not evolved into its positive state, the ability to feel genuine remorse for mistakes, also is a cause of brain chemical imbalance. It triggers the brain's release of tryptophane-induced beta-endorphins. They are forty-eight times more powerful than an equivalent dosage of morphine. Autopsies performed on people driven to suicide by chronic depression have revealed levels of beta-endorphins up to two hundred times the maximum tolerance level for morphine.

Experiencing a wave of negative shame also causes a surge of electricity in the brain which burns out its electrical circuits. Severe physical or emotional pain causes physical damage to the brain's systems in a similar way.

Another causation of such disorder is an infant's too rapid switch from the crawling stage to walking. If a baby doesn't experience bilateral crawling—an arm moving in unison with the opposite leg—the corpus callosum, a "highway" of nerve fibers connecting the two cerebral hemispheres which allows smooth interaction between them, doesn't develop properly. Dyslexia and similar learning disorders often result.

Some of us made a choice after birth to be spectators in this lifetime—losers sitting on the sidelines—either because we came in under the influence of some past-life childhood trauma, or because an early experience in this childhood was too terrible. In order to fulfill a promise made to ourself to not consciously participate in creating our reality, we had to distort our brain mechanics or alter our brain chemistry.

A malfunction in our nervous system may have been caused in infancy or childhood because we were unable to get enough dream-sleep for complete brain and nervous system development. Constantly being awakened in infancy or childhood, perhaps by well meaning relatives or by ill health, may have caused the lack of sleep. Children who dread sleep for some reason are also unable to dream sufficiently.

We may have experienced any combination of these sources of brain malfunction, but in most cases, the problem with our holographic brain can be corrected in meditation.

Continually identifying our boundaries and working to expand and transform them moves us forward in our growth process. Limiting beliefs are changed into positive, more expansive beliefs. Obstacles are replaced with ideals, principles, and character. Hope takes the place of contracts we've consciously ended. Old scripts are replaced with dreams and visions of a positive future. Through meditative techniques, distorted brain chemistry and mechanics are made whole.

These steps of personal growth lead the way for spiritual growth.

CHAPTER 9

Becoming Whole

Becoming Whole

*I*n our human experience, we have been bruised and battered in lifetime after lifetime. We have been misdirected and have gotten lost. In order to become whole again and to set ourself back on course, we need to understand how to heal our emotional wounds and how to find our Real Self.

EXPLORING HUMAN EMOTIONS

The origin of emotion lies with the Goddess and God. Love was the first, and it will be the final emotion for us all. Love is the basis of all creation and it is the voice which calls us Home. *Everything* we do is done from a need for, a yearning for love. Love is an expansive emotion. It has no boundaries. Love is the essence of our Soul. It is the glue that holds all of reality together.[30]

The vast range of all other human emotions stems from love. As we infinitely downstepped our energy, moving farther and farther away from our Source, there emerged a second emotion—loneliness.

In the grand order of creation, wherever there is expansion, there is also contraction. The explosion of Creation

121

was an expansion of Devine Love. Loneliness, a contracting emotion, is felt when there is a sense of disconnection from God/Goddess/All That Is. That *first* loneliness is the same loneliness we now have when we feel far removed from love.

Out of a further contraction of loneliness, came the emotion of *fear*. Fear of being cut off forever from that love. Fear of being alone. Fear of loneliness.

Born of that original fear, in places farthest from Home, there emerged all other fears. Fear that we could not love good enough to return Home. Fear of our inadequacy. Fear of failure. Out of our primal fears evolved anger, hurt, pain, jealousy, envy, rage, sorrow, hatred, remorse, despair—and the spectrum of contracting emotions.

There are no right or wrong emotions. No good or bad emotions. There are just *emotions* and we are meant to experience them all—and to learn about ourself from them. That is the process which will allow us to drop away, one by one, the contracting emotions until, at the higher levels, we will be left with only expansive emotions like passion, compassion, gratitude, happiness, joy, and love. We cannot yet comprehend the intensity of those emotions.

Emotions, therefore, are an important component in human and spiritual development.

In our present reality, created by the imbalance of masculine energy over feminine, emotional expression—a feminine principle—is devalued. Certain emotions also are judged by the consensus to be bad, or *negative*, and we are reluctant to even acknowledge that we have them. Children are taught early to suppress the emotions that make others uncomfortable.

As a child, when we perceived that we had been abandoned, betrayed, abused, or otherwise wronged, there arose natural feelings of pain, anger, fear, even hatred and rage. We, the child, misdirected those feelings, turning them inward instead of aiming them at the offender, most often a parent. We did so because it is too frightening to a child to vent strong emotions toward the adults upon whom their survival depends, and also because it is the nature of children, until about the age of ten—in their naiveté, to believe that *they* are the cause of everything that happens to them.

As adults, we often rationalize away those childhood experiences and emotions—they happened so long ago it doesn't matter anymore. Or we believe that there is nothing we can do to change the past, so we must try to make the best—or worst—of it. Those approaches set the stage for replaying over and over past experiences and the emotions they produced.

Ignoring stuffed emotions from childhood is an ineffective way of dealing with them and it keeps the wounded inner child trapped in the past. That child is still a part of us. It is unable to become a healthy *free* child because it has never been given the opportunity to release pent-up feelings.

The child's emotions were stuffed deep inside and covered with a balm of self-pity or martyrhood. That is how we survived the otherwise unbearable pain, fear, and anger, but those original feelings have never left us.

Until repressed feelings are acknowledged, expressed, and released, they will continue to negatively impact our life. We will subconsciously continue to create cycles of behavior, relationships, and circumstances in order to give ourself new opportunities to deal with them.

If intense emotions continue to be suppressed, for we learned as a child that was the only way to handle them, they often erupt in our reality in an explosion of violence. We get feedback from our world—personal and global— about the intense feelings we've stuffed down into our Shadow Self and about our own potential for violence that we refuse to admit is there.

With courage and brutal honesty, we can own and process those hidden parts of ourself and thus diffuse them.

Processing emotions not only includes expressing and releasing them, it also means forgiving. Forgiving ourself for having created the negative reality in the first place and also for not dealing with it sooner. Forgiving the offender, not necessarily for what they did to us—some things were too damaging to be forgiven—but for *why* they did it.

Parents who wrong their children were themselves wronged as children. That does not excuse what they did— they had a responsibility to heal themselves rather than to pass along their shame, rage, and pain—but it does explain the *why* of what they did and that can be forgiven.

We resist forgiveness because we have misconceptions about it. We believe that it absolves the other or makes them right and us wrong. We believe forgiveness is a sign of weakness or that only a higher authority has the power and the right to forgive.

Children don't have the emotional or mental capacity to be responsible for creating their reality. They are neither equipped for dealing with their deepest emotions nor are they capable of self-healing. As our adult self, we can assume the responsibility for healing our wounded inner child and adolescent. That gift of freedom and love will change our life.

It is easier to deal with emotions when we understand them.

Positive and Negative Emotions

The consensus views emotions such as love, happiness, joy, and compassion as positive. It gives us permission to express them—within reason. Emotions like anger, hurt, jealousy, and fear are considered negative and therefore undesirable. We are encouraged to ignore (suppress) those feelings for they are uncomfortable to have and awkward to deal with in others.

Many popular philosophies for self-healing and spiritual growth suggest that we should simply transform anger, jealousy, fear, hurt, and other such "negative" emotions into love.

Our most intense emotions—the depths of hatred, rage, pain, and despair—are too frightening, even to mental health professionals, to encounter head-on. We are treated with drugs to mask and further suppress them.

The problem with these approaches is that *all* emotions must be and will be processed. They will not go away by themselves no matter how much we deny them.

If we do not consciously acknowledge and express our emotions, they will process themselves automatically—frequently as illness. Emotions give us valuable feedback that lets us know there is something blocking our personal and spiritual growth.

Anger is the feeling most frequently suppressed. Although we try to hide it, we fool no one. We send out a vibration of anger which impacts our reality. Other people feel it. It is not hidden by the smile on our face. The resonance of the emotional vibrations we emit attracts like vibrations. The resonance of unexpressed anger sets up a potential avalanche of negativity which can bury us—by "one thing after another."

Silent anger is used by martyrs as a manipulation and as a punishment. If we consciously try to replace our anger with love, as we're told we should, the love comes out as a sticky-sweet goo and is unconvincing. Sugar-coated anger is one way we create a phony persona and with it block intimacy in our relationships.

As our real self, with real emotions, we will attract and be attracted to other real selves. That will result in honest relationships with people who know and trust us and whom we know and trust.

All emotions are positive when they are consciously acknowledged and appropriately expressed. It is only when we deny, suppress, and repress them that they become negative emotions for that is when they cause us damage. When love is denied—either the giving or the receiving of it— it becomes a negative emotion just as does anger denied.

Love, the original expansive emotion, is more than a feeling, it is a powerful force and it is also a process composed of specific actions to be taken for the purpose of producing particular states of being. It is important that we first learn to love *ourself*, for it is only then that we are capable of truly loving others.

The actions of the love process are: *giving* generously in ways appropriate to the circumstance; *honoring our own emotions* by expressing them and honoring the other's emotions by permitting their expression; *responding* to our own needs and those of the other; *knowing* ourself and knowing the other; *being humble* enough to allow ourself, or the other, to be different this time from the way we or they always have been in the past; having *courage enough to make a commitment*; honestly *caring* about the welfare of ourself and the other.[31]

Each of the actions in the process of love is to be taken for the purpose of producing any or all of these states of being: having a sense of *security*; feeling *pleasure*; being honest and therefore *vulnerable*; *trusting*; having a *reduced fear of loss*; feeling *intimate and cared for*; being *known*.[32]

In the process of love, the steps of getting there produce the state of being there.

Real and Unreal Emotions

Real emotions, either expanding or contracting, are those which have both a positive and a negative aspect, depending upon whether or not the emotion is expressed. Love, anger, fear all have both positive and negative sides to them.

Of all the real emotions, shame is perhaps the one with potentially lifelong tragic impact.

There are four waves of shame[33] which come at intervals in our lifetime. The first comes in infancy, the second in childhood, the third in adolescence, and the fourth can come at any time in adulthood.

From birth to about eighteen months of age, an infant is symbiotically linked to its mother. It has no sense of being separate from her. It feels totally deserving and cries until its demands are satisfied. During this early period an infant needs unconditional love—having all of its needs met in a compassionate and loving way—in order for healthy development.

From about eighteen months to around three years of age, the child begins to break down the symbiotic relationship it has with its mother in order to learn about the world. It discovers it is separate from mother and everything else—a joyous and frightening and exciting discovery. The first wave of shame begins at this time in childhood with an infant's first attempts at independence.

As the child tries to make its own way as a newly liberated individual, it makes mistakes. It is necessary for healthy development that this early break should occur, and the shame felt for mistakes is meant to evolve into remorse. Learning remorse goes along with learning that it is permissible to make mistakes. Being allowed to make mistakes and to feel genuine remorse for them produces a free child, one of the components of a healthy adult.

But often something happens during this period which prevents the shame from evolving into remorse and the shame gets repressed instead. The repression of shame alters a child's brain chemistry by triggering the release of too many endorphins—painkillers. In infancy, the brain is too new and a flood of endorphins—an overdose—can burn out neuronal structures and nerve endings.

The repression of shame during the first wave is caused in four ways: by a mental, emotional, or physical abandonment by one or both parents; by any kind of abuse; by being wronged through excessive or unjustified scolding or punishment; or by being taught to deny the shame and remorse the child feels. If shame is repressed at this time, the child not only feels shamed—it senses that it *is* the shame.

The second wave of shame comes in childhood between six and eight years of age. During this time, the child once more begins to move away from mother, this time toward father. The shame will again be repressed if there is any kind of abandonment by father or if either parent dumps their own shame onto the child by expressing subhuman behavior (any type of abuse) or superhuman behavior (demanding that the child *do* or *be* as good as the parent). Shame is passed from generation to generation in this fashion.

Around the time of puberty, from about ten to thirteen years of age, a child moves away from father toward peers. That emotional and psychological shift begins the period of adolescence in which the third wave of shame occurs.

As devastating as infant and childhood shame was, it is much more so in adolescence. The causes of shame—superhuman or subhuman parents, abandonment, abuse, being wronged—has more impact because the adolescent understands more fully the implications of such treatment. The effects are longer lasting for the adolescent is robbed of the ability to clearly perceive, conceive, think and feel, and to know their own needs and wants. They are robbed of their ability to imagine, to heal, and to love—all the gifts of being human. Now the brain chemistry, altered by earlier waves of shame, floods the body with endorphins and raging hormones. Tape-loops of learned behavior are programmed into the brain, setting up the automatic future replication of the abuse, abandonment, and wrong done to the child or adolescent. Life decisions, contracts, and scripts are established at this time.

The fourth wave of shame comes at any time in adulthood. It is the time when shame is most likely to be passed on to others. Most shame-based adults dump their own shame onto children.

Other adults come to peace with their shame and accept the remorse that lies behind it. It is possible to free ourself of shame in adulthood by processing it, then meditatively giving it back, perhaps as a smelly sack of garbage, to those who dumped theirs on us.

Shame accumulates, but each wave of shame can be dealt with and we can be free of it. There are reference materials in the Resources section of this book which offer methods for dealing with shame.

Shame, painful as it is, is a real emotion when it evolves into remorse. Remorse is the positive aspect of shame.

Unreal emotions have only a negative aspect. Guilt does not have a positive side and it is not a real emotion. Underneath guilt is anger that we feel we do not have a right to have, and therefore will not allow ourself to feel. Having guilt is one way we give ourself permission to continue the guilt-producing behavior.

Inducing feelings of guilt in others is a way to manipulate them, and a way to control them.

Harboring guilt or using it against others is not conducive to personal and spiritual growth. We can eliminate guilt by recognizing it and then by identifying and processing the underlying anger.

Anxiety has no positive aspect and it is not a real emotion. Anxiety camouflages real emotions like anger, fear, hurt, and self-pity which we have not acknowledged. It also appears when we anticipate rejection, humiliation, or failure. We feel anxiety when our trust is misplaced.

Anxiety is dangerous for it sets up a potentially fatal resonance. Its force is so destructive, it can bring serious illness or even death.

The positive way to handle anxiety is to first identify which of the underlying causes it is hiding. That done, the real blockage can then be processed and released.

Depression is not a real emotion. It is a disguise for anger which we have suppressed because subconsciously we believe that we will get into trouble for having it.

There are two types of depression. One type is caused by any event, positive or negative, which brings about sudden and unexpected change. For instance, a job promotion from out of the blue can cause depression.

Often new mothers experience depression. Though anticipated, the birth of the baby causes a sudden and (in some ways) unexpected change—like loss of freedom. But how can a new mother be angry? She is supposed to be overjoyed. Her hidden anger, along with hormonal shifts, can produce serious post-partum depression.

Any sudden and unexpected change causes a kind of chaos and a sense of loss of what was—and that triggers anger. When we suppress that anger, it produces depression. It is a natural reaction and if we get to the underlying anger and express it, our depression will end.

The second type of depression, chronic depression, is brought on by the piling up, over time, of layer upon thin layer of small unidentified angers and hurts. Finally, one last straw—usually an insignificant thing—brings on an onslaught of depression. This type of depression is more harmful because it is deeper and longer lasting. When we suffer chronic depression we become incapacitated by it and are unable to process the underlying angers and hurts. Sources of help for healing this type of depression are listed in the Resources section.

Acknowledging and expressing the full range of human emotions adds depth to our life. When we are willing to experience deeply all of our emotions, we will be able to experience the intense love, joy, passion, and compassion that are elements of personal and spiritual fulfillment.

FINDING OUR TRUE SELF

Following the path of our personal and spiritual growth, as we handle the obstacles which stand in our way, as we let go

of our emotional ties to the past, as we learn to acknowledge and express our feelings, we will also find and become
our True Self, for that is a necessary part of the process.
Our True Self is the traveler who is heading Home. It
is our *adult* self who owns their true value.

The Adult

An adult is the product of a synergy of the free child, curious adolescent, nurturing parent, and positive ego aspects
of a grown-up human being.[34]

It is the inherent nature of a child to want to be loved
perfectly, to be loved completely and unconditionally. That
is not possible of course, but under the best conditions, the
child will get *enough* unconditional love from outside
sources to evolve into a healthy *free* child. That joyous
aspect of ourself will be carried forward to help us learn
how to have fun as we continue to mature.

When we reach the age of about thirteen, our adolescent self emerges. It demands to be understood totally. In
ideal circumstances, the adolescent will be understood
enough to placate its unfulfillable need and will become the
healthy *curious* adolescent. It is another component which
we will bring forward into our adulthood where it will help
us find self-understanding.

As a grown-up, ideally, we learn to handle our negative
ego and are left with a positive ego which simply delivers
messages about our reality so that we may respond to them.
We learn to be our own nurturing parent, who provides for
and protects us. With these components, we are a true adult
—with the freedom of a child, the curiosity of an adolescent, a positive ego, and being our own nurturing parent.

What most often happens, however, is that somewhere around four, five, six, perhaps seven years of age, the child aspect of ourself gets stuck in time and space. Any of the factors which produce shame—abandonment, any type of abuse, betrayal, being wronged by superhuman or subhuman parents—any childhood trauma, so impacts the child that it cannot move forward until it is healed. Instead of the free child, we carry with us as a grown-up, that wounded inner child.

The adolescent, crippled by childhood wounds, stumbles into its time of rampant hormones and insecurities. Without the help it needs to understand itself and its place in the world, the adolescent suffers its own wounding. It, too, gets locked into time and space, refusing to evolve until it gets the healing it must have.

Eventually, our body matures, but with our child and adolescent stuck in the past, we do not automatically become an adult. Instead, our wounded inner child and inner adolescent become very adaptive. We can appear to be adult, we look the part, we have successful careers, get married, have children of our own, but it is our inner child and inner adolescent who take turns playing on our adult stage.

It is not possible for a child or adolescent to take responsibility for creating their reality. They lack the emotional and mental capacity to do so. For that reason, a grown-up who is not coming from their adult self will not have what is required for significant personal and spiritual growth. The key that unlocks the door to such growth is held in the hands of the adult.

When an adaptive child and adolescent are leading a grown-up life, they need supervision. We bring in the critical parent aspect of ourself to berate, to punish, to frighten, to lay down rigid laws, for we learned from the consensus of authority figures in our life that that is how we must control our behavior.

Without an adult us to monitor it, our negative ego runs rampant, delivering messages to us of our superiority or inferiority and all the other lies it is compelled to tell.

There is another influence to deal with which hampers our growth into adulthood.

Generally speaking, the predominance of male chauvinism in the world creates a climate which encourages men to remain in their adaptive child or adolescent stages throughout their lives, while women act out the critical parent. The roles are switched from time to time. but the overall pattern stays in place.

If we wish to grow, we need to bring forth our adult self, first by making the decision to become an adult, then by handling the components which are taking its place, so that we can assume conscious responsibility for creating our present reality—then we are free to make it the reality we dream of.

As our adult self, we can more fully discover our personal value.

The Valued Self [35]

The first component of self-value is *self-awareness*. That is the awareness that we have *impact* on everything in our reality and that our reality, in varying degrees, has impact on us.

Many of us learned as children, from the reactions of our parents, that we only had negative impact and so we decided early on to go through life having as little impact as possible—or denying that we had any at all. But it is important for the development of our self-value to understand that what we say, what we do, what we think, and also what we *don't* say, do, or think has impact, in some way, on *everything* in our life. Equally important, is the acknowledgment and understanding that everything *out there* has mental, emotional and/or physical impact on us.

Another component of self-value is *self-worth*. That is the worth that is given—the worth that we automatically have because we are a piece of God/Goddess/All That Is. Our worth doesn't have to be earned, only acknowledged and received. Each of us has worth equal in measure to all others. In that way, we *are* all born equal.

Self-esteem is the third aspect of self-value. Self-esteem is the compassion and caring we have for ourself that we earn through our personal honesty, integrity, responsibility, and trust, the internal sources which no one can take from us. It is quite different from esteem which comes from outside sources such as material possessions, friends, fame, physical appearance, titles, education. These can all be wonderful creations in our reality, but if we use them as our source of self-esteem, it will lack substance and stability. That type of self-esteem cannot sustain itself and must be constantly replenished, for it is insatiable.

Self-love, like self-worth, is an aspect of self-value which is given. Self-love is the compassion and caring that is given by God/Goddess/All That Is. We are loved by God/Goddess/All That Is unconditionally and They know our name. They love us as the unique spark of consciousness we are. There is nothing to prove to get that love. We do not have to earn it. All we need to do is discover it and to let the love in. To accept it, to receive it, to *be* loved by God/Goddess/All That Is.

The fifth component of self-value is *self-confidence*. Self-confidence is the knowledge that we, as a singular person, can skillfully cope with life no matter what happens. It is a learned skill and awareness that evolves with practice, with trial and success or error.

We need to understand that it is all right to make mistakes. That is why we created time and space in our physical illusion. Rather than seeking perfection, as so many of us do, we need to allow ourself to take risks, to try new things, new ideas. Failure is only an indication of a faulty belief. *We* are not a failure simply because what we tried did not bring the desired results. Whenever we learn something about ourself, we do not fail. That self-knowledge contributes to our self-confidence.

Self-respect, the sixth aspect of self-value, comes from honoring our emotions—acknowledging and expressing them appropriately as they arise. (See Exploring Human Emotions, this Chapter.)

The last component of self-value is *self-realization*. It is the state of being which is produced by the synergy of the other six components. It is the whole that is greater than the sum of its parts.

The synergy of our self-worth, self-love, and self-respect forms the essence of our Divinity. Our self-esteem, self-love, and self-confidence synergisticly create the essence of our Humanity.

As with the process of love, discovering and integrating each of the components of self-value produces the state of *having* self-value.

The exploration to develop the adult self who knows its personal value might include sources of information suggested in the Resources section at the end of this book.

The adult with self-value is the True Self each of us

can become. That Self already exists, for we have many levels of consciousness, each in its own time-space. All we need do is evolve into our existing True Self as we travel our path.

CHAPTER 10

The Old Paradigm: Clinging to the Past
A New Paradigm: Reaching for the Future

The Old Paradigm: Clinging to the Past
A New Paradigm: Reaching for the Future

*J*ust as there are parallel physical realities, there are parallel models, or paradigms upon which those realities are based. The paradigm accepted by the consensus to explain how physicality works evolved in the 17th Century. It is a linear paradigm founded upon the concept that *the past creates the present.*

In 1687, the English mathematician and philosopher, Sir Isaac Newton, published Book I of his *Principia* which contains what are known as Newton's Laws of Motion. One of his axioms, "To every action there is always an opposed and equal reaction," is a theory of mechanical cause and effect which was scientifically correct in certain defined circumstances, but which became broadly adopted to explain how all of physicality works.

Newton's theory does not allow for variety, freedom, and chaos. It does not allow for spontaneity or miracles.

With the publication of Books II and III expanding his laws to include the power of gravity on the planets and their moons, Newton's single set of laws became the physical and intellectual foundation of the modern world. The *Encyclopedia Britannica* declares the *Principia* as "perhaps the most powerful and influential scientific treatise ever published."

Logic, commonly valued as *correct* reasoning, is defined as the necessary connection or outcome of cause and effect. Reason and logic, based on linear past-creates-present cause and effect, are the only yardstick by which the consensus measures the validity of beliefs and behavior.

Another influential body of work was produced earlier in the 17th Century by French philosopher and mathematician, Rene Descartes. Descartes' philosophical stance and perceptions about science also relied on a rigid mechanistic concept of the physical world.

Descartes determined that human beings were separate and distinct from the rest of the universe, thereby making them *observers*, not participants, and further, that the human mind and brain were separate from each other. His duality theories became the model for scientific research.

Descartes' demand for certainty and his narrow view that the validity of any belief must depend on its ability to be proven by logic and rational reconstruction of thought still has impact upon modern culture and most schools of modern science.

Newton's and Descartes' inflexible theories from the 17th Century are the foundation of the consensus's current belief system. They place the power of reality creation in forces existing outside the human being. They leave no room for occurrences which cannot be proven. The illogical and unexplainable—paranormal—things which happen are denied official scientific recognition.

The old paradigm is not the highest truth and has never been. We believed it was the only truth and labored to find a reason from the past for everything that happened in the present. It was our *belief* which made it true.

The old paradigm relies upon the concept of linear time—seconds, minutes, hours, days, weeks, months, years, and so on—and supports our beliefs about crime and punishment, virtue and reward, sin and retribution, heaven and hell. That is why it is an integral part of organized religion. Indeed, linear time as we know it was established during the period when the world's major religions were being formed.

In the totality of human experience, linear thinking is actually a very recent approach to dealing with physical reality. Before logic and reason were valued so highly over imagination, feeling, and intuition, the world was regarded quite differently.

Prior to the linear concept, time was seen as cyclical—measured by sunrise and sunset, waxing and waning of the moon, changes of season. The Earth and the elements were integral aspects of time. In that way, time was an ally in harmony with the universe. People understood the unbroken thread of birth, death, and regeneration as it applied to all of nature. A kinship was felt between humankind and all of the realms in the Physical Plane. Everything was known to be an aspect of consciousness—minerals, plants, animals, and planet Earth, herself. That was a time when we had dominion in the world.

As we moved away from dominion, we sought, instead, domination over our environment. We forgot our fluid connection to nature and established a different order based upon rigid structure, upon laws and rules.

The consensus has tenaciously held on to beliefs in inflexible rules, laws, and established order in physical reality out of an underlying fear of the chaos which would exist without them. We want physical matter to be *real*. We want to *prove* that it is. But we cannot, for we live in a hologram, an illusion, of our own design.

Most certainly there is a kind of chaos in a reality created without rigid rules and laws, but there is chaos with them as well. If we do not take conscious responsibility for creating our reality, it is a dark chaos manifested by what is submerged in our subconscious and unconscious minds. We can no longer dominate our physical reality. We can no longer control it. The condition of our world tells us so.

If we do take responsibility, the darkness becomes light. A light chaos where miracles are allowed. A light chaos where we consciously create what we want and don't have to *prove* how we do it, and yet its manifestation *is* the proof. The light chaos is filled with paradox, yet from it emerges the reason and order we seek.

The old paradigm no longer works for our world. In it, there are no solutions to many of the world's problems. The new paradigm is the only way out of them.

Discoveries about atoms and subatomic particles, of which all physical reality is composed, began a school of science in the early 1900's known as quantum physics. Those discoveries decisively refuted the Newtonian/Cartesian model of mechanical physical reality by, among other things, showing that an electron (a sub-atomic particle) could make a quantum leap from one place to another without passing in between. Niels Bohr made that discovery, and later another—that although the world appeared to be continuous, it was fundamentally a discontinuous and quantum-jumping world.

Although Albert Einstein played a major part in the development of quantum physics, he ultimately became its foremost critic. Einstein's famous Theory of Relativity proposed that time/space was the fourth dimension and therefore had impact upon the other three.

Einstein argued until his death in 1955 that there must be an undiscovered order to physical reality—that the observer is separate from the observed. He called it "objective reality." Subsequent theories and discoveries by quantum physicists have proven, over and over again, the concept of objective reality to be wrong.

Quantum physicists, more than sixty years ago, discovered in laboratory experiments with subatomic particles that the expectations of the person performing the experiments impacted the results of the test—"subjective reality." Werner Heisenberg's Principle of Uncertainty signaled the end of the mechanical universe for it showed that the universe changed whenever the observer altered the way they observed it. It was found that radiant energy, a photon, could be either a stationary particle *or* a moving wave, depending upon the belief of the observer and therefore the test given.

In our universe, all energy moves by wave action. When we focus our attention on it, it stands still. That is how we create our holographic reality. The simple test with a photon explains the mystery of it all.

The focus of our Mind—conscious, subconscious, unconscious—creates our reality and also how we experience it.

In the old paradigm, where it is the past that creates the present, the focus has been on the past and trying to fix it. The famous saying about those who do not learn from the past being destined to re-live it, is more accurately stated as, Those who focus on the past, are destined to recreate it.

The new paradigm is about focusing on the future, for it is the future which creates the present. That is a higher truth. As we set our sights on the future we want to create for ourself and the world, we do in the present what is necessary to reach that future.

The past is merely the backdrop for the present. It is no more concrete than the future. History has been written then revised again and again, always reflecting the personal perspective of the historian who writes it. For that reason, there are many different accounts of the same historical events. In our personal life, family members often recall past events differently. The past is as variable as the future.

Outside of the four lower levels of consciousness—the Physical, Astral, Causal, and Mental—which we have created, time and space do not exist. All time is now. The past has no more *weight* than the present or future. It is we who have given it weight in exchange for abnegating our responsibility for creating our current reality.

Responsibility—the ability to respond *and* to take action—is the key to changing reality. Responsibility is the foundation of the new paradigm.

Our personal reality appears to be continuous because we belong to a "set" co-created with others who share our beliefs. Individually, we can jump sets—taking a quantum leap into a new reality—by taking responsibility for creating our present reality and changing ourself based upon the feedback we're getting from it. In that way we can jump from the set of the old paradigm into that of the new.

The new paradigm is not about achieving perfection.

God/Goddess/All That Is continue to evolve, to become *more*. In that sense, They are not perfect, for perfection is a static state. It signifies the end of growth. The continuing evolution of God/Goddess/All That Is is our guaranty of conscious immortality.

The new paradigm is about focusing our attention

upon the future we want to create for ourself and our world; and doing so by creating a present that will take us there. It is the *means* that justify the ends.

When we align the energies within ourself, focusing more and more on the future, less and less on the past, we create a resonance which will set the tone for the future. When we allow ourself to receive what is new and use imagination, desire, and expectancy to shift our beliefs, attitudes, thoughts, and feelings toward the future we personally want for ourself and the world, that is how we will create it.

Because everything is a matter of choice, we are not forced to create a new future nor to experience the new paradigm.

There are those unwilling to step into it or even to allow it. Many are desperately clinging to the past, clinging to the old paradigm, and they are creating a reality without a hopeful future. The past *is* their future. Many are exiting the planet to avoid it. Many believe the world is ending and manifest it so for themselves.

Every one of us creates our own reality. No one else does it for us. In that sense, we are all alone in our hologram. But, paradoxically, we have also allowed others into our reality so that we could experience *impact*—ours upon them and theirs upon us, for without it, we could not learn about compassion and love. The awareness of impact is the first step toward self-value.

Love is the most powerful emotion, the most powerful force, action, and state of being. Unconditional self-love will enable us to successfully and joyfully exist upon those higher levels of consciousness where there is no cushion of time and space. Where every thought will manifest instantly. As we evolve, self-love and love for others will replace our contracting emotions and without them, we will not create the situations which produce them.

The holographic reality we manifest in the new paradigm is the expression of our growing self-love. The old paradigm is created from a lack of it.

God/Goddess/All That Is have given us total freedom of choice—with one suggestion, Do what thou wilt, with harm to none.

By creating our reality out of self-love, with harm to none, as we focus on the future of our ideals, hopes, and dreams—we cannot go astray. Success is guaranteed.

The new paradigm will rely upon new and lighter societal systems and institutions. The old establishments will be replaced. They are already crumbling as the shifting now takes place. Governments are changing and falling. Religions are being shaken from within. Scientific establishments, including medical science, are changing. Academia is changing. Corporations and commerce are changing. The old systems are falling away, making way for the new.

The human brain is also transforming.

Our brain's temporal lobes interpret the messages our five physical senses deliver to them. Our temporal lobes have been calibrated by the old cause and effect belief system, calibrated by thousands of years of male chauvinism, therefore they have allowed us to perceive our reality only as it conformed to those calibrations.

The obsipital lobes in our brain, which allow us to see our reality, receive what has been filtered by our temporal lobes. The visual images that our eyes see conform to our temporal lobe calibrations. Our eyesight, our vision of physical reality, is limited in that way. As we shift into the new paradigm, our temporal lobes are being re-calibrated by the electro-magnetic energies in our environment in a way that will allow us to perceive reality differently.

The vortices of electro-magnetic energy being generated more powerfully and more frequently now around the world, resulting in increased tectonic activity, storms, and other natural occurrences, are also impacting—changing— our brain's temporal lobes.

EM energy is a raw force that exists *between* the realities. It is a common area between the Earth, a living consciousness, and all other consciousness. Within the common area, a communication is occurring. The communication is at the level of the unconscious mind. We each have a single unconscious mind for all of our lifetimes and our unconscious mind is in touch with those of all others.

The communication within the collective unconscious mind of planet Earth, of humankind, and of other entities within the Physical Plane is for a purpose of mutual benefit— the creation of a new physical reality, a new world, a new universe.

One way the communication is being manifested on the Physical Plane is by thousands of so-called crop circles— actually quite elaborate in design—which are symbols meaningful to our unconscious mind. The crop circles are created by EM energy directed by the collective unconscious mind as a communication to our singular unconscious mind. At higher levels of ourself, we are allowing this to occur. Aerial photographs of just ten of the many crop symbols which appeared in England in 1994 are included in this chapter.

The crop circle/symbols are also telling us that true magic and miracles are real and that physicality is an illusion. Their appearances in areas around the world cannot be explained by any scientific means despite the many efforts to do so. And they continue to appear, though the consensus *chooses to ignore them at this time.*

Through the crop symbols and through the EM energy itself, the evolution of our holographic brain is occurring.

Electro-magnetic energy increases the receptivity of our brain's temporal lobes and also its capacity to imagine.

With a more highly evolved brain, those who so choose will be able to create a future reality far beyond our present ability to imagine. That future world will be manifested from the *Imaginal Realm*. It is a realm where Imagination imagines itself. It is based on a truth higher than "I create my own reality." References to information on this important development appear in the Resources section.

The thousands of crop symbols which have appeared in certain areas around the world, increasingly since 1990, have great meaning to our unconscious mind for they tell of the shift in paradigms and of the return of the Goddess and Her love.

Our body's immune system is another structure undergoing significant change. It is breaking down and will be replaced by a new and improved immune system. Increased longevity will result.

Our old belief systems are changing as well. The changes are manifesting now as the deterioration of the infra-structure of cities and countries, built so long ago, as the breaking apart of political systems and blocks of countries.

Each of us experiences these changes differently. For many the experience is quite painful. The Resources section of this book offers sources of insight and help for dealing with these personal and global changes.

The present chaos will be followed by more than just a new world order—there will be a new world.

Cheesefoot Head, Winchester, July 1994   *(Photo © Steve Patterson)*

Devizes, Wilts, July 1994   *(Photo © Steve Patterson)*

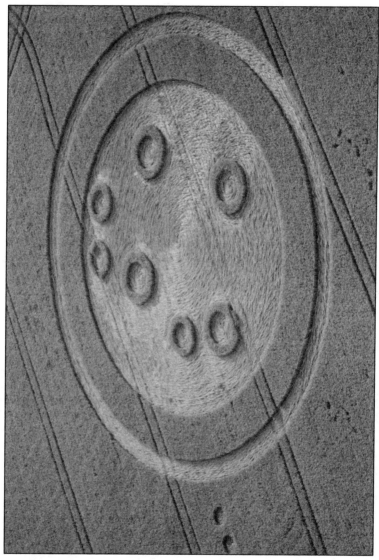

Froxfield, July 1994   *(Photo © Steve Patterson)*

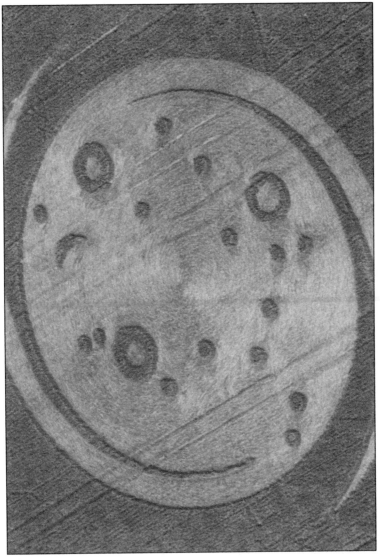

Alton Barnes, Wilts, July 1994   *(Photo © Steve Patterson)*

Alton Barnes, Wilts, August 1994   *(Photo © Steve Patterson)*

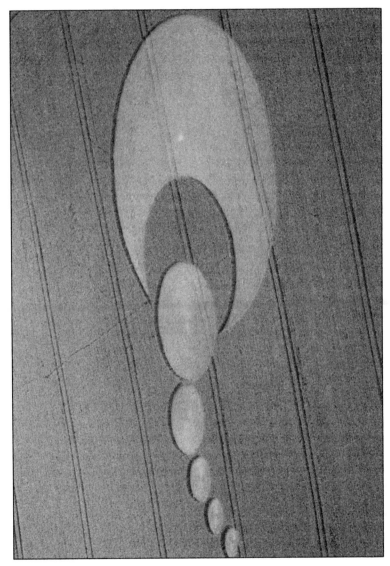

Oxfordshire, August 1994   *(Photo © Steve Patterson)*

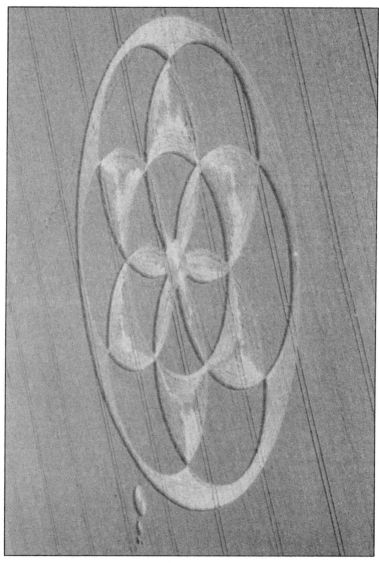

Froxfield, August 1994   *(Photo © Steve Patterson)*

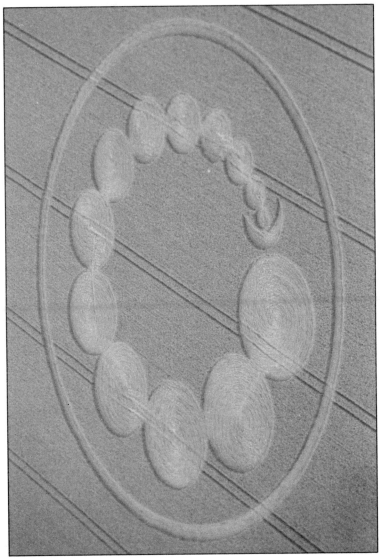

Avebury, Wilts, August 1994   *(Photo © Steve Patterson)*

Avebury, Wilts, August 1994   *(Photo © Steve Patterson)*

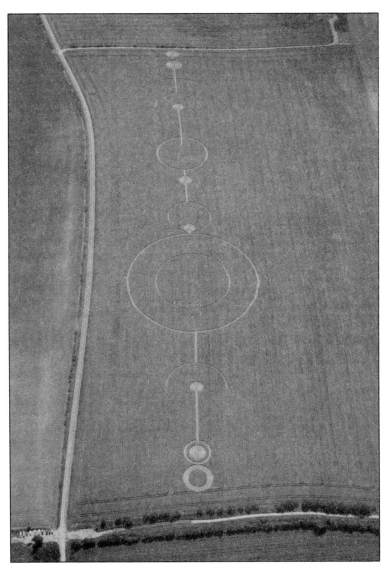

Uffington, Wilts, August 1994   *(Photo © Steve Patterson)*

We are being drawn into the new paradigm by the Goddess. She creates the space and She provides the light that will lead us into it.

There is a grand symbol of Her light and love standing in a harbor on the shores of America. America, itself, is a symbol of the compassion, freedom, and self-determination of the Soul and the Spirit of humankind.

The multiple evolutions taking place at this time— each multi-layered—are creating a chaos which many fear for they do not understand it. Some see the chaos as a prelude to the end. It is often easier to envision, even hope for, total destruction in one fell swoop to clear the way for what is new. That is the adolescent's way of bringing about change.

But evolution does not require painful destruction. Evolution can be gentle. We can make it so through self-awareness and understanding; through personal transformation.

As we change internally, there will be less external demonstration of the need for change. The outward chaos is feedback shouting loudly about what we need to attend to within.

The brilliant future we create will be a return to having dominion in our world, living in harmony with our environment. Rather than past-to-present linear causation, we will bring it about by downward causation—from the psychic and spiritual levels of ourself.

That spiritual connection is a powerful force. When we tap into it and use it, the future we can manifest is unlimited. And so are we. Unlimited by the despair and disease of body, mind, and spirit.

We can extend our life for as long as we choose—if we are willing to assume that responsibility for ourself. We can allow discoveries, treatments, and inventions in the scientific world which will provide assistance for longevity, but first comes the personal responsibility for our own healing.

The events of the 1960's were a harbinger of what will come. Change occurred in many ways during that time when peace and love were so promoted. However, it was a time without personal responsibility. Peace and love were the wishful desires of the inner child and adolescent, incapable of taking responsibility. Love was defined by the masculine mind set of chauvinistic society. The bright prospects of the 1960's tarnished and were lost.

As we now bring forth and become our adult and valued self, as we seek the balance and harmony of our masculine and feminine energies, we give peace and love a power that will prevail.

People with personal power and self love are a threat to the structures of the consensus. But we must remember that it is we who create that reality.

It is *we* who create the imbalance of masculine and feminine energies. *We* who allow the consensus of male chauvinism to establish the norm. In lifetimes past, we were the ones who created the imbalance and we are the ones who maintain it now—not religion, not government, not the consensus.

By balancing our internal feminine and masculine energies as we reclaim the power we gave away, by loving ourself first, making us able to truly love others, by forming an equal partnership between men and women—in these ways we will create a societal consensus that resonates at a higher frequency. A consensus that sees it normal to be loving and compassionate, normal to live in peace and harmony with fellow human beings, normal to be in dominion with nature and the universe.

As we seek fulfillment of our focuses using the feedback of our reality for guidance, as we consciously seek and expand our spiritual connection to God/Goddess/All That Is, as we change personally—that is how we will change our present and future world.

The Goddess is patiently waiting. As we turn toward Her, She beckons us to join Her in the brilliant future of a new world.

Her light will show the way.

Her light will lead us Home.

ENDNOTES

Chapter 1

1. The author's description of creation is based upon her personal understanding and interpretation of the teachings of certain being-friends, including Lazaris.

Chapter 2

2. Throughout this chapter, the author's description of the evolution of consciousness is based upon her personal understanding and interpretation of the teachings of certain being-friends, including Lazaris.
3. Lazaris has discussed at great length the specific components of reality creation briefly mentioned here.
4. See Note 6 below.
5. See Note 6 below.
6. Lazaris has discussed at great length the concepts of *human animal, human being,* and *first directional lifetime* which are briefly mentioned here.

Chapter 3

7. Lazaris has suggested that these two focuses are chosen by each of us for every lifetime.
8. These are some of the emotional strengths identified by Lazaris.

Chapter 4

9. The author's description of Lemuria, which follows, is based upon her personal understanding and interpre-

tation of the teachings of certain being-friends, including Lazaris.

10. The author's description of Atlantis, which follows, is based upon her personal understanding and interpretation of the teachings of certain being-friends, including Lazaris.

11. M. Gimbutas, *The Civilization of the Goddess: The World of Old Europe* (New York: HarperCollins, 1991.)

12. See Note 11 above.

13. See Note 11 above.

14. See Note 11 above.

15. See Note 11 above.

16. The author's description of female chauvinism, in this chapter, is based upon her personal understanding and interpretation of the teachings of certain being-friends, including Lazaris.

17. The author's description of male chauvinism, in this chapter, is based upon her personal understanding and interpretation of the teachings of certain being-friends, including Lazaris.

18. The components of feminine energy briefly discussed in this chapter have been described in great detail by Lazaris. The information presented in this book is the author's interpretation based upon her understanding of the material.

19. The components of masculine energy briefly discussed in this chapter have been described in great detail by Lazaris. The information presented in this book is the author's interpretation based upon her understanding of the material.

Chapter 4

20. See note 19 above.

21. See note 18 above.

22. Lazaris has offered this definition of the Highest Truth.

23. See Note 11 above.

24. See Note 17 above.

Chapter 6

25. The author's condensed explanation of the Faces of the Soul and the phases of human development, presented in this chapter, is based upon her personal understanding and interpretation of the teachings of certain being-friends, including Lazaris.

Chapter 8

26. Lazaris has suggested that these components create our initial human developmental boundaries.

27. These specific clues to martyrhood have been offered by Lazaris and discussed by him at great length.

28. Lazaris has offered these four components of trust and has discussed the subject in great detail. The author's brief explanation of trust set forth here is based upon her personal understanding and interpretation of the subject.

29. The author's description of the Negative Ego is based upon her personal understanding and interpretation of the teachings of certain being-friends, including Lazaris.

Chapter 9

30. The author's discussion of the origin and evolution of emotions, presented in this book is based upon her personal understanding and interpretation of the teachings of certain being-friends, including Lazaris.

31. Lazaris has offered these components of the process of love as specific actions to be taken to produce specific states of being.

32. See Note 31 above.

33. The author's condensed explanation of the four waves of shame, presented in this section, is based upon her personal understanding and interpretation of the teachings of certain being-friends, including Lazaris. Extensive taped discussions of each wave of shame are available in the materials listed in the Resources section at the end of this book.

34. The components of the Adult Self briefly discussed in this chapter have been described in great detail by Lazaris.

35. The components of the Valued Self briefly discussed in this chapter have been described in great detail by Lazaris.

True wealth is having access to resources.

—Lazaris

Suggestion:
If you don't know where to begin,
ask your Higher Self for guidance.

RESOURCES

The following materials have been resources for the author in her quest for personal and spiritual growth.

Abundance and Prosperity: The Skill*

Accelerating the Pace of Manifesting Success*

Achieving Intimacy & Loving Relationships (Video)*

Activating Miraculous Success*

Ageless Body, Timeless Mind, Deepak Chopra, Harmony Books, Publishers, 1993.

AIDS: At the Hay House*

Awakening the Heroes Within: Twelve Archetypes to Help Us Find Ourselves and Transform Our World, by Carol S. Pearson, HarperSanFrancisco/ HarperCollins, Publishers, 1991.

Awakening the Love (Video)*

(The) Backdrop of Success: a Whole New Fabric of Being*

Balance: Releasing the Full Self (Masculine and Feminine Energies)*

Being Loved*

Beyond the Threshold/Editing the Film*

Breaking and Replacing the Dark Shield (#6012)*

Building Your Personal Dream, Part I (#7010)*
Building Your Personal Dream, Part II (#7011)*
Busting & Building Ego*
Busting & Building Image*

Chakras/Pituitary-Pineal Meditation*
(A) Cherished Secret of Success: Resonance (#7025)*
(The) Civilization of the Goddess: The World of Old Europe,
    by Marija Gimbutas, HarperCollins, Publisher, 1991.
Closer to the Light: Learning From the Near-Death
    Experiences of Children, by Melvin Morse, MD.,
    with Paul Perry, Ivy Books, Publishers, 1990.
Conceiving/Perceiving*
Conquering Fear*
Consciously Creating Success*
Crafting the Life You've Always Wanted*
Creating, Building & Keeping Intimate Relationships*
Creating the New Play*
Crisis of Martyrhood*
(The) Crisis Tape (#6017)*
Crystals: The Power and Use*

Developing a Relationship With Your Higher Self
    (Video)*
Developing Self-Confidence*
Developing Self-Confidence (Video)*
Discovering the Adult*
Discovering Your Subconscious*
Discover the Dreamer from Lemuria (#6010)*
Dominion at Work: Engaging the Elements*

Earth Energy/Earth Power*
(The) Elegance of Abundance: The Art of Having It All*
Embracing Your Higher Self: Receiving the Love
   (#6000)*
Ending Guilt*
Ending Loneliness*
Ending the Frustration of Hidden Agendas*
Ending the Pain*
Ending Self-Punishment*
Ending Self-Sabotage*
Ending Shame, Part I (Infancy)*
Ending Shame, Part II: Psychic Contracts of Pain*
Ending Shame, Part III: Those Adolescent Years*
Ending Shame, Part IV: Adult Shame*
Escaping the Entrapment of Perfection*
Escaping the Suffocating Web of Anxiety*
(The) Evening Tape (#6020)*
Excellence*

Fear: The Internal War*
Feeling More of Lazaris' Love: Blending (#7002)*
Forgiving Yourself (Video)*
Freedom From Self-Pity*
Freedom From the Past (#6021)*
Freedom From The Unspeakable: Jealousy, Envy, Rage*
Freedom: Its Mystery and Power*
(The) Future: How to Create It (Video)*

(The) Gentle Walk: Intimacy with Your Higher Self*
Getting More Magic Out of Meditations (#7000)*

(The) ghost in the atom: a discussion of the mysteries of quantum physics, by P.C.W. Davies & J.R. Brown, Cambridge University Press, Publishers, 1986.

(The) Goddess: Beginning to Receive Her (#6024)*

(The) Goddess Series, Phase I: Preparing to Meet the Goddess*

(The) Goddess Series, Phase II: Opening to the Initial Faces of the Goddess*

Gratitude*

Handling Depression/Handling Loneliness (Meditation)*

Happiness*

Happiness/Peace (Meditation)*

Harmony: The Power Vortex (Masculine and Feminine Energies)*

Harnessing the Power: Magically Ending Martyrhood*

Harnessing the Power of Your Destiny*

Healing Hurt/The Keys to Happiness*

Healing the Adolescent Within (#7014)*

Healing the Child Within (#7013)*

Healing: The Nature of Health, I*

Healing: The Nature of Health, II*

Hearing the Music...Allowing the Magic (#7016)*

High Energy/Enthusiasm (Meditation)*

High Magic: The Ritual of Receiving (#6022)*

(The) Holographic Universe, by Michael Talbot, Harper Collins, Publishers, 1991.

I Deserve!*

Improved Health/Balance & Harmony (Meditation)*

(The) Incredible Force of Foregiveness*

Inner Peace*

Integrity/Honesty (Meditation)*
Intimacy*
Into the Deep: Realizing Unrealized Power*
Intuition*

*Lazaris Interviews: Book I**
*Lazaris Interviews: Book II**
Lazaris Talks With Vietnam Veterans*
Letting Yourself Be Loved: Allowing Lazaris' Love
   (#7008)*
Listening to the Whispers (Video)*
Living Magically Everyday*
Longevity: The Healing Tape (#6007)*
Loving*

(The) Magic of Joy*
(The) Magic of Relationships*
(The) Magic of Receiving: A New Dimension of Success*
(The) Magic of Our Spiritual Heritage (#6014)*
Making This Your Last Lifetime*
Mind Meld: Higher Self (#7018)*
(The) Mists of Manifestation (#6008)*
Monetary Success/Personal Success (Meditation)*
(The) Morning Tape (#6016)*
(The) Mysteries of Empowerment (Video)*
(The) Mysterious Power of the Chakras*
(The) Mystery and Magic of Co-Creation*

Negative Ego: Ending the Co-Dependancy*
(The) New Age Begins*

(The) New Age and Its Future
a.k.a. California Consciousness II*
New Dynamics of Processing/Programming*

(The) Omega Project: Near-Death Experiences, UFO Encounters, and Mind at Large, by Kenneth Ring, Ph.D., William Morrow and Company, Inc., Publishers, 1992.

On Releasing Anger/On Releasing Self-Pity*
On Releasing Guilt/On Receiving Love*
Opening the Magic Door (#6002)*
Orin and DaBen materials, Luminessence Productions.
Our Secret Prison: Discover and Break the Dark Law*
Overcoming Fear of Success (Video)*

Owning Your Own Shadow, by Robert A. Johnson, HarperSanFrancisco/HarperCollins, Publishers, 1991.

Personal Depth: Health, Wealth & Success*
Personal Excellence (Video)*
Personal Power & Beyond (Video)*
Personal Power/Power & Dominion (Meditation)*
Positive Ambition*
(The) Power & Beauty of Self-Acceptance (#7021)*
(The) Power of Dominion*

(The) Power of Your Subconscious Mind, by Dr. Joseph Murphy, Prentice-Hall, Publisher, 1963; Bantam Books, Publisher, 1982.

Productivity/Impeccability (Meditaiton)*
Programming What You Want*
Prosperity & Abundance in the 1990's*

Reality Creation: The Basics*
Receiving the Healing from Your Higher Self (#7012)*

Reducing Fear/Worry/Stress (Meditation)*
Relationships the Work*
Releasing Negative Ego (Video)*
Releasing Your Dreams & Visions Into the World
  (#6011)*
Renewing Chakras (#6026)*
Responsibility & Freedom*

(The) Sacred Journey: You and Your Higher Self (Book)*
(The) Sacred Journey: You and Your Higher Self
  (Meditation Tapes)*
Secrets of Manifesting What You Want, Part I (Video)*
Secrets of Manifesting What You Want, Part II (Video)*
Secrets of Spirituality I*
Secrets of Spirituality II*
Secrets to Changing Anything in Your Life-Instantly*
Self-Confidence/Self-Awareness (Meditation)*
Self-Esteem*
Self-Love/Love (Meditation)*
Self-Worth/Self-Respect*
Sharpening Tools: Awakening Desires (#7001)*
Spiritual Mastery: The Journey Begins (Video)*
*(The) Spiritual Seekers Guide: The Complete Source for
  Religions and Spiritual Groups of the World,* by Steven
  S. Sadleir, Allwon Publishing Co., 1992.
Stop Feeling Not Good Enough*
Stop Negativity in Its Tracks (#6015)*
Stumbling Blocks/Building Blocks*
(The) Synergy of Trust*

Taking the Quantum Leap: The New Physics for Non-Scientists, by Fred Alan Wolf, Harper & Row, Publishers, 1981.

(The) Tapestry of Success*

Testimony of Light, by Helen Greaves, Neville Spearman Publishers, 1969, latest reprint 1991.

Thirty Years That Shook Physics: The Story of the Quantum Theory, by George Gamov, Doubleday & Company, Inc., Publishers, 1966.

Transforming Personal Fear Into Amazing Success*

(The) True Magic of Waking Up & Staying Awake*

(The) True Power of Success*

Turning Potential Into Achievement*

(The) Ultimate Relationship*

Unconditional Love (Video)*

Unlocking Creativity*

Unlocking the Power to Change Your Life (Video)*

Unlocking Your Unconscious (#6013)*

(The) Unseen Friends*

Utilize the Unknown Powers of the Magical Child*

Utilizing Solstice & Equinox Energy (#6003)*

Utilizing the Incredible Mystery & Magic of Expectation*

Waking the Magician: Sacred Return to Oneness*

(The) Wheel of Eternity, by Helen Greaves, The C.W. Daniel Company Limited, Publishers, 1974, Reprinted 1988.

Winning the Manifestation Game*

Winning: New Tools to Get What You Really Want*

(The) Woman's Encyclopedia of Myths and Secrets,
   by Barbara G. Walker, HarperSanFrancisco/
   HarperCollins, Publishers, 1983.

(The) Young Adult*

Your Uniqueness*

Your Future Self*

---

*by Lazaris (audiotape, unless designated otherwise);
Concept: Synergy/NPN Publishing. Available through
your local metaphysical bookstore.

INDEX

Crystal Cities, 41
Crystal, 41, 46
Curiosity, 71, 82-83, 87, 132
Curious Adolescent (aspect of
    adult self), 132
Current life, 19

D

Dark Ages, 68
Dark chaos, 79, 144
Dark Law, 79-80
Dark shadow, 82
Death, 21, 31, 61, 66, 84, 92, 117,
    130, 143, 145
Decision, 18, 32, 34, 36, 83, 86,
    91, 109, 115, 129, 134
Dense, density, 16, 22
Depression (emotional, mental),
    117, 130-131
Descartes, Rene, 142
Desire, desiring, 13-15, 35-36, 40,
    47, 51-52, 63-64, 115-116,
    147, 162
Despair, 122, 125, 161
Destiny, 0, 25, 27-29, 31-33,
    35-36, 108
Destroyer (energy), 80-81
Deva, 92
Digestive tract, 20
Directional lifetime, 165
Disease, 161
Divinity (self-worth, self-love,
    self-respect), 10, 136
DNA, 17
Do, doing (masculine principle),
    51, 53
Domain, 17, 40, 92

Domination, 10, 49-50, 62, 91,
    143
Dominion, 47, 49, 91, 143,
    161-162
Double (face of Soul), 82-83
Downstep, 13, 15-16, 19, 21, 92,
    121
Downward causation, 161
Dream, 16, 40, 44, 48, 94, 114,
    116, 118, 134, 148
Dream-sleep, 114, 118
Drug, 44, 81, 125
Druid, 45
Duality theory, 142
Dwarf star (Sirius B), 16
Dyslexia, 117

E

Earth, 16-17, 39, 45-46, 61,
    92-93, 143, 149
Earthquake, 43
Eastern Religions, 30, 61
Ego, 22, 36, 110-111, 132, 134,
    167
Egypt, Egyptian, 45-46, 64-65
Einstein, Albert, 144-145
Electro-magnetic (energy/fields),
    93, 149-150
Elegance, 14, 84
Elements, 29, 47, 61, 80, 92, 131,
    143
Elohim, 65
Elves, 92
EM energy (See Electro-magnetic),
    93, 149-150
Emotion, 20, 30-31, 33, 49, 52,
    58, 80-81, 85, 94, 96, 104,

Male-oriented God, 59, 63

Man's world, 50-51

Manifest, manifesting, 8, 13, 16, 18, 32, 43, 48, 50, 52, 78, 80, 82, 94-96, 116, 144, 147-150, 161

Manipulate, manipulation, 49, 78, 107-108, 126, 130

Martyr, martyrhood, 28, 33-34, 44, 51, 78, 106-108, 113, 123, 126, 167

Masculine energy/principles, 13, 37, 39, 41-43, 45, 47-53, 57, 61, 64, 71, 96, 122, 162, 166

Masculine, 13, 37, 39, 41, 43, 45, 47-53, 57, 59, 61, 64, 71, 96, 122, 162, 166

Masculine mind set, 59, 162

Master (energy of adolescence), 78-79

Matrilineal culture, 64

Mayan, 45

Media, 58

Medical science, 148

Meditation, meditative, 35-36, 40, 63, 76, 82, 85, 92, 95, 97, 105, 118

Mediterranean area, 48, 64, 66

Mental, mentality, 16, 20, 58-59, 77, 82-84, 95-96, 110-111, 124-125, 128, 133, 135, 146

Mental health professionals, 125

Mental Plane, 16, 95-96

Messenger, 32, 98

Metaphysical, metaphysician, 44, 60, 92

Michael (archetype/fire), 92

Middle Ages, 67-68

Middle East, 45-46, 66

Milky Way, 17

Mind, 14, 18-19, 29, 35, 41, 58-60, 68, 76, 80, 82, 84-86, 95, 97, 105, 110, 142, 145, 149-150, 161-162

Mineral kingdom, 22

Miracle, 66, 115, 141, 144, 149

Mistake, 30, 32, 112, 117, 128, 136

Modern world, 59, 141

Mohammed, 68-69

Molecule, 21-22

More, 9-10, 14-17, 21-23, 27, 29-32, 34-36, 39, 42-45, 48, 53, 58-59, 62, 65, 68, 70-71, 75, 79-80, 82-83, 86-87, 92, 94-97, 99, 103, 107, 113, 116-118, 126, 128-129, 131, 134, 145-147, 149-150

Morphine, 117

Moses, 65-66

Mother (aspect of the Goddess), 71

Mother, 1, 58, 66, 71, 77, 113, 127-128, 131

Motivate, motivating, motivation, 10, 15, 22-23, 107-108, 115

Multiple lives, 19

Myth, mythology, 45, 66

N

Naive One (energy of childhood), 77

Name (face of Soul), 68, 76-77, 97, 135

Negative ego, 36, 110-111, 132, 134, 167

W

Waif (energy of childhood), 77-78, 80
Warrior (aspect of Goddess), 60, 71
Water (element), 17, 44, 92-93
Wave action, 16, 145
Wave of shame, 112, 117, 128-129, 168
Weakness, 124
Western Religions, 64, 69
Wisdom, 3, 8, 41, 71, 83-84, 98
Wise One (energy of old age), 83
Wiseacre (energy of old age), 83-84
Women, 27, 47, 50-51, 60, 63-65, 68-69, 109, 134, 162
World, 7-9, 18, 22, 27, 29, 31-32, 39-41, 43-44, 46-51, 57-62, 64, 68-69, 76-77, 81-82, 84, 92-93, 107, 112, 124, 133-134, 141-144, 146-147, 149-150, 161-163, 166
Worth, 14, 92, 135
Wounded adolescent, 80, 111
Wounded child, 106, 111, 123-124, 133
Wounding (face of Soul), 79
Wronged (in childhood), 106-107, 122, 124, 128-129, 133

TO ORDER COPIES OF THIS BOOK

Please send this order form or a photocopy of it to:

> IMDEX Publishing
> P.O. Box 5283
> Huntington Beach, CA 92615-5283

Sales Tax: California residents add 8.25% sales tax.

Shipping: Book Rate: $1.25 for first book
plus .50/each additional book
First Class: $2.25 per book

Payment: **PLEASE INCLUDE CHECK OR MONEY ORDER
PAYABLE TO IMDEX PUBLISHING**

Name: _____

Street: _____

City: _____

State: _____   **Zip:** _____

Price/Book: $12.95 or $12.45 for 5 or more copies

x number of copies (_____) = $_____.____

(California residents) **Tax:**   _____.____

Shipping: _____.____

Total enclosed: $_____.____